The Project Fixer
A Leadership guide on the art of becoming an Un-f*cker

M. Eric Ritter, PMP

Copyright © 2019 M. Eric Ritter

All rights reserved.

ISBN: 9781674568447

DEDICATION

For anyone who has ever fallen. For anyone who has been defeated. For anyone who got back up, dusted themselves off and tried again. This book is dedicated to those who have the inner fortitude to persevere against the odds. Rise to the top not to prove to others that you can, but because you would never accept less for yourself.

CONTENTS

	Introduction	i
1	The Problem With Problems	1
2	Logical Thinking	11
3	Own It	20
4	Plan for Failure	28
5	No Matter Where you go, There you are	32
6	How does an Ant Eat an Elephant?	43
7	Nerds, Geeks, the Artsy-fartsy types and Millennials	58
8	I want to be the Emperor (empirical data rules!)	78
9	It's not you, it's me	87
10	Are we there yet?	107

INTRODUCTION

It's a strange title, but entirely descriptive. I can't guess at how many times I've been told; "I'm so f'ed, this program is f'ed," etc. I've made a career out of being able to fix these broken efforts. I've learned enough over more than 30 years of military, contractor and civil service employment to write a book. Then a friend said, "You should write a book". So, here we are.

There are plenty of books out there that tell you the right ways to do things. Tons on project management, business management, service management, you name it. Everything is all about how you should do things from the beginning. But what about the business projects that didn't follow those great processes? These projects tend to end up in serious trouble. How do you un-fuck this mess? Where are those books?

I don't expect this book to be a how-to guide for every situation. This is not a step-by-step book professing to be the one solution to all your problems. It's an honest look at the causes and possible solutions, to problems. I'm hopeful that I can convey the strategies, qualities and methodologies that have been successfully (and in some cases not) employed to, well, fix stuff. To keep it from being too dry, I'll share some stories along the way. One thing I do strive to do is include real-life examples and situations you may face, and concepts, practices and tactics to deal with them.

A quick note on my stories- They are just that: Stories. Mostly true, but don't think of them as statements of fact. The point is to illustrate an idea or provide background to real life situations that might help the discussion. Dates, places and people might not be exact, but it won't take away from the intent of the message.

Be forewarned- I use plain talk, and sometimes I talk

like a sailor. This book will contain some language that might be offensive. I'll keep it to a minimum, but I'm an old sailor and this is the way I talk. I didn't want to write a book that didn't come from the heart, so I decided to write it the same way I would say it if we were in a bar enjoying a beer. Or five.

Ron White: "What's my favorite beer? Usually the fourth one. Duh."

One of the most important concepts that you will hopefully learn in this book is that people working together toward a common goal is a very powerful thing. When these people get along together it can be extremely rewarding. Consider this:

Shared happiness has the effect of multiplying. Tell a good joke, share a smile, a special event or even a simple good deed. The people around you will share in the joy, and often spread it further. Conversely, shared sadness is divided. When you seek comfort from the people around you, share a frustration, a setback, even a loss, they pick up some of the load. Soon, you feel some of the pain is relieved. Maybe not all of it, but certainly enough that you feel a little better.
"Shared joy is multiplied; shared misery is divided"
Thanks to Spider Robinson for putting to word my long-held belief

Are you ready to become a Fixer?

CHAPTER 1

THE PROBLEM WITH PROBLEMS

Let's go back a long time ago. In 1982, I joined the Navy. I was 22, really interested in engineering, electronics and puzzles. And bored to tears. I wanted to travel and see the world. I wanted somebody (other than me) to pay for it. To shorten what could be a long, drawn out story, I ended up becoming an Electronics Technician. The important thing here is that part of the training for this job is what the Navy calls Basic Electricity and Electronics school, or as every sailor called it- B Double E. B/EE took you from simple concepts of electricity and prepared you for the much more challenging specialty schools. In my Case, Electronics Technician (ET) "A" school.

While in B/EE, we were taught one of the most important lessons I have ever learned. It's called the six-step trouble shooting process. This was, to me, an eye opener. The Navy had devised a process that could find any problem in an electrical based system, circuit or component. Cool. Here- it seems simple, right?

The six steps of troubleshooting.
1. Identify the problem.
2. Establish a theory of probable cause.
3. Test probable cause theory to determine actual cause.
4. Establish an action plan and execute the plan.
5. Verify full system functionality.
6. Document the process.

The thing here to realize is that this is a process. Imagine you are responsible for fixing a broken radar repeater (the screen). On a ship. At sea. In a storm. Your boss is standing over you. There's 20,000 volts DC floating around in there somewhere. Oh yeah...you're at war and missiles might be inbound- but the ships radar repeater is broken, so you don't know. Quick. Un. Fuck. It.

It sure would be nice to have a process that has been pounded into your head so that you would simply "do" and not have to decide *what to do*. It's like athletes who do skills thousands upon thousands of times. They get "muscle memory". They act and react automatically. When someone yells "Get your head in the game!", they really mean get your head OUT of the game. Let your training take control. Don't think-DO. Having a process enables that behavior. It works in less stressful situations, too.

A primary tenant of the 6-step process is that you need to understand how things work when everything is performing as designed. Step 1, Identify the Problem, needs you to be able to say that the system (program, device, car...whatever) isn't working the way it's supposed to. How can you know if something is wrong if you don't know how it behaves when everything is right?

Zoom ahead for a few, to 1994. I'm still in the Navy, but working as a computer tech. A glorified Help Desk person, to be honest. A customer, a high-ranking officer, would call up and complain, very upset, about their computer not working. Going to their desk side and being dutifully respectful as they deride the horrible IT services that they are expected to live and suffer with on a daily basis, I set to figuring out how I can help. As a matter of fact, I started by asking "How can I help to make your day better?" I found that most irate people find it difficult to be an ass toward you when you are kind and understanding. Psychological Reciprocity. I told him that I was sure that his issue was frustrating. I shared that, I too, get frustrated when things don't work the way I expect them to. Then I started asking some questions. The first thing I would need to do was establish if there was a problem. Not what *was* the problem. Many times, there was a screw loose in the operator. For example, his complaint was that "every time I use my word processing program the damn thing won't let me save the file". After discussing the issue with him, I discovered that the file names he was trying to use aren't recognized by that word processor program. It wouldn't allow dashes (-). In other words, there was no problem- the system worked the way it was designed to. That didn't make the customer happy, but it saved me hours of trying to fix a problem that didn't exist in the first place.

When looking at the big picture of resolving problems, no matter what they are, the first thing to consider is if you know how things are supposed to work. If you don't, or you aren't certain, find someone who does. Surround yourself with Subject Matter Experts (SME's). Your Internet search engine might be enough of a SME for you or you may need to find an owner's manual or even a system designer. Whatever it takes, don't sell yourself as being able to fix anything if you don't understand how that thing should be working when it is fixed.

If you can't tell me exactly what you want, I can't be sure I'm able to give it to you.

This concept extends way beyond a computer or car or some device. It goes to the root of nearly everything ever. The way something is designed to perform, whether it is an item, a system, a process a relationship, or even an organization. If you need to Un-Fuck something, you had better be sure you know how it must be performing when you are done. If you don't know exactly what the outcome is expected to be, how will you ever know when you are done? Think of it as requirements gathering.

Howie Mandell: "What do you do for a living?"
Audience member: "Nothing."
Howie Mandell: "How do you know when you're

finished?"

How do you identify a problem? The most common methodology is when outcomes are not reaching expectations. You press down on the accelerator and you expect the car to go faster. If that doesn't happen, you start searching for the problem. What's the first thing that you do? My guess is that you use your senses to detect something out of the normal. Did you hear your engine respond to the extra gas? Do you smell anything funny? Did you feel a skip, lurch, shimmy in the car? Did you notice the "Check Engine" lamp on? You probably go through all these things automatically. What you are already doing is part of step 1 of the process. You are looking for fault indicators to help identify a problem. But wait a minute...

Are you looking for a problem or a symptom? Symptoms are not the problem. They are indicators. Think like a doctor. Symptoms point us in the right (hopefully) direction to the root cause of the problem. When a patient presents with itchy eyes and sneezing, the doctor may treat the symptoms with some antihistamine. A good doctor will identify the source of the allergic reaction and recommend the patient to avoid the irritant. In other words, the good doctor will resolve the actual problem and return the patient to proper working order.

In our car example, the symptom is the car not accelerating as expected.

1985, on liberty with a fellow sailor. We're in my car driving from Norfolk, Va. to New Rochelle NY. My car is more than a few years old, but he wants to visit family and I don't have anything better to do. So, we do what shipmates (or any other service members) do. I offer to drive him there and enjoy the comradeship. There is a bridge that goes over the Delaware river. We have stopped for gas, chips and some barley sodas (not proud, but honest). This bridge is big. Way up. No problem, of course.

Until we're about 10% up the hill and I start smashing down on the gas pedal and the car isn't responding. Jim and I are yelling at each other-WTF??- people in the cars behind us are beeping and my car won't go over 12 mph!! We seriously considered getting out to push (no way, on the uphill side of the bridge? There may have been a few beers in that thought process), but we decided that would be too much like work. Besides...we were at least moving - slowly. With a couple dozen angry motorists enthusiastically encouraging us forward.

When we crested the bridge, it was like magic. Suddenly the car had life again. We whooped with joy, hitting a glorious 55mph on the down-hill ride. Once off the bridge, cars whipped around us, saluting as they passed- most only using one of their fingers. As we headed further on the road, although the car seemed to be working okay, I noticed the check engine lamp was on. Crap. An indicator for sure, but overall pretty useless. Something was still wrong, but now the only symptom was that damn light.

We got a few more miles into New Jersey when we had to go up another (much smaller) hill. The car began the same thing. Throttle fully depressed and the car just didn't go any faster. It was time to suck it up. We had a real problem. Pulling over to the side of the road was a good idea. Taking the beer cans out of the back seat and putting them in the trunk was a great idea. When the state trooper pulled up behind us we were relieved. He couldn't help us though and had to call a tow. We were poor sailors. All the money we had was for food, beer and a hotel room. Crap.

When we got towed to the nearest repair shop the guy did something totally unexpected. He said; "Thank you for your service, Semper Fi!" and drove off. This wasn't something we were used to, being pre- 9/11. We wanted to thank him back, but he was off before we could even think. Unfortunately, the repair shop wouldn't be so generous. The catalytic converter had crapped, and it was several hundred to get repaired. I ended up calling Navy Federal Credit Union and they deposited a loan into my account that paid for the repair and a little more. The bad news is we wouldn't have enough time to make it to his family's home. But since we were more than halfway to Atlantic City...

The check engine lamp wasn't the problem. The lack of acceleration wasn't the problem. They were symptoms. When the symptoms went away (going down the hill) we were happy. But the problem was still there.

Therefore you, as an Un-F*ker, must know the difference between the symptoms of a problem and the root problem. It happens often that the only indicators of a problem are the symptoms. In business, we often see situations that lead us to knee-jerk reactions. When things are running behind schedule, work longer hours, bring in more staff; and yet, many times that doesn't get things back on track. What was actually causing the symptoms to manifest themselves?

In 2010, I was the Program Manager (contractor) supporting the Operations Division within Consular Affairs at the State Department. I was responsible for the IT departments systems engineering, web services, asset management and communications contracting staff. When I came aboard, the government client was frustrated. A major event each year is the State Department's Diversity Visa Program. To give you an idea of the scope of this annual event, in 2010, there were 9.7 million visa applications submitted. Submissions in 2007 were 9M, 2008 was 10M, 2009 was 13M. Something was wrong. What happened? Why the sudden drastic down turn (yes, a one year drop of 3 million was drastic)?

When I asked the people running the program what they thought the problem was I got some interesting answers. The client (State Dept officials) said the contractors must have messed up somewhere. They aren't delivering what is expected. The contractors (various companies) were quick to point fingers at each other, all claiming "not my fault". The electronics systems supporting the event appeared to be working, although logs indicated very heavy utilization. All of these things were symptoms of the problem, not the actual problem.

Determine what, if anything, has changed, since the system last worked properly, which may have caused the problem. Importantly, before you take any action, if possible, make a backup copy of the system, so that you can preserve everything as it is.

In my discussions with the various people involved in the setup and operations of the system, I asked, "What was changed from last year?" I learned that a new contractor team had come in, that there had been changes to how the form was submitted by the applicants, and that the intake system had been upgraded to allow for more space and faster processing.

In previous years, applicants would fill out a written application form and submit it to their local (in their country) U.S. Consulate. The form would be scanned and sent electronically to be entered in the system for evaluation, and possibly issue a work visa. There was an inherent problem with this methodology. The Diversity Immigrant Visa Program (DV Program) makes up to 50,000 immigrant visas available annually, drawn from random selection among all entries to individuals who are from countries with low rates of immigration to the United States. These countries are typically (not exclusively) made up of what we would call third-world countries. Many have poor to little technical infrastructure. That was certainly the case in 2010. Hopefully there has been improvement since then, but the point is this: In many countries, people who wanted to apply lived many miles from the US Consulate. They did not have access to the forms nor did they have good transportation.

Imagine someone living in abject poverty, dreaming of coming to the US, and learning that there is a way they might be able to do that. She saves everything she can for a year and then must make a trip of over 400 miles to get to a consulate. She walks, runs, gets rides in a wagon, and eventually makes it to the city. She's never been in the city and feels lost, scared and confused. When she walks up to the consulate, a US Marine is who she must face first. He's intimidating, but nice, and directs her to the line of a hundred or so people who are already waiting to submit their applications.

Once inside, she has to fill out the application. Hopefully, thankfully, she had all the proper credentials to answer all of the questions. She even had the pictures that would be used to issue her visa if she was a winner in the lottery. She finally hands her completed application to the clerk who adds it to the tall stack of others. Exhausted, she now has to make the trip back home to wait, and pray, that she might one day be coming to America.

There had to be a better way, right? The entire system was invented to help the most underserved individuals in countries that didn't get a lot of visas granted. In the US and most first-world countries, we would never put up with a process like this. So why did we make it so hard for them? The State Department put together some great minds and concluded that it was time to modernize the process. Instead of making the poor people go to the consulate, we can just let them submit their application online. No more standing in line, no traveling all the way to a consulate, no waiting to find out your application was rejected to some error. Sounds great, right?

Wrong. The primary symptom (low submission of Visa applications) wasn't the root cause problem. The problem was that the people trying to apply didn't get the message that things had changed. They didn't have access to mass media. They didn't have access to computers. If they did get access to a computer, it cost money to use. It cost money to get on the Internet. The connections were so poor that many people couldn't fill out the forms before being disconnected. If they were lucky enough to press the submit button, many times the systems wouldn't connect to the State Departments download system because the connections were so poor or to slow. When we analyzed the system logs we discovered huge amounts of dropped connections. So, what was the root cause of the problem? It's probably not what you think.

The concept of modernization of the system was a good idea for so many reasons. It made it easier to submit applications. It resulted in fewer rejected applications due to the system not accepted incomplete or improperly filled forms. It should have simplified things on the State Departments end by having everything electronically submitted and not having to be entered into the system from a scanned form. It would reduce staffing requirements, time to execute, provide better statistical data and many other tangible benefits. The pictures and biographical data would be accessible to facial recognition systems and law enforcement agencies. So what was the problem?

I questioned the customers/stakeholders.

I remembered that the symptoms were not the underlying problem

I considered what had changed

And then I moved on to **Step 2. Establishing a Theory of Probable Cause**

CHAPTER 2

LOGICAL THINKING

"He had a better mind and more rigorous temperament than me; he thought logically, and then acted on the conclusion of logical thought. Whereas most of us, I suspect, do the opposite: we make an instinctive decision, then build up an infrastructure of reasoning to justify it. And call the result common sense."
-Julian Barnes

When you understand how a thing, system, organization, whatever, works when it performs as it should, you should be able to identify areas that could, theoretically, be the problem. To illustrate the point, let's say you have a home entertainment system. It's composed of a smart TV, a sound bar, an Audio/Video Receiver, a cable or satellite box and all the wires that connect them, plus the universal remote. Everything works the way you set it up. When you click "Watch TV" on your remote it launches a macro program that turns on your TV and selects the Video 1 input. It turns on the receiver and selects Video 1 output and sets the volume at 4. It turns on the cable box and selects channel 112. All is right with the world. Then, one day that doesn't happen. Your TV doesn't have a picture!

Do you pick up the phone and call the cable provider to find out what's wrong? Maybe eventually, but if I'm right, you will check some things first to figure out a theory of probable causes. What's most common in cases like this? You might check the remotes batteries. You would check to see if the A/V receiver, cable box and sound bar are on. You look to the TV to see if the power light is on. Would you go to check your circuit breaker box to see if a fuse is blown? Probably not. At least not yet. Because it's not the most likely cause. Definitely a possible cause though. But consider that another possible cause could be a nuclear war broke out and nobody told you. The point is we are looking for probable causes. You are using logical thinking.

Okay, so let's make a list. In this situation, you'd do it in your head. In real-life business situations you should write it down.

- Is each piece of equipment power on lamp lit?
- Is the system set to the proper inputs/outputs?
- Do I get a picture if I change the channel?
- Are the cables firmly attached?
- Did I pay the cable bill?

These are pretty easy things to check. In this case, you should pick the easiest things to check first and by process of elimination, determine what the problem is. If you eliminate everything from the list, you may need to consider other, less likely causes (the fuse box?) or possibly escalate to a higher authority (the cable company?).

The point is, we don't just start tearing apart the sound bar looking for a loose wire. It isn't logical. That would be a waste of time, resources and might even break the sound bar. I call it Easter Egging, because it reminds me of three-year-old's running every which way to find an egg. They have no rhyme nor reason where the look, just hoping they will be lucky and find an egg.

Another problem you have to watch out for is jumping to conclusions due to experience. Just because you have seen the same symptoms before, don't assume the problem cause is the same.

In the real world of complex business problems, we have to do a little more work. When you create a list of the probable problem, you need to use your understanding of what the desired/designed performance is supposed to be. It's often helpful to put your list in order of most to least probable. Logically identify areas that could result in the issue you are seeing. If a car keeps slipping gears, it's not logical to examine the airbags systems. The point is, don't Easter Egg. Use your brain, your understanding of how the system works.

Based on your Theory of Probable Causes, Identify Possible Faulty Functions

Use logic to identify and to eliminate possible faulty functions. If the power strip lamp is on, you can eliminate the circuit breaker from the list. If all power indicators are on all the devices, it no longer makes logical sense to be a power issue. Cross it off the list. Now your list is smaller. The remaining checks and tests may be more difficult to verify or test, but eventually you will get to the thing that is causing the problem.

Wrong is easy (why troubleshoot when they already did it?)

In 1996 I was teaching members of the Navy Recruiting Command's team of system administrators. I would go to recruiting districts around the country and teach basic trouble shooting to people who had no real training in IT. Most of the time, they were pretty computer savvy users. At one such event I was asked to help resolve a problem that had been stumping the onsite technician for quite some time. The customers were irate at this point and the support staff was feeling the pressure. When I was asked by the Commander in charge to see if I could help, he directed me to a Chief Petty Officer who oversaw the IT team.

The first thing the Chief wanted to do was to tell me everything that they had done to try to resolve the problem. I can tell you that I forever blew any chance of becoming friends with this chief. I told him that I don't want to know anything he and his team did to try to fix this problem. Why? Because you failed to fix the problem. Why should I believe anything that you did to be true? The fact is, if you did everything right, the problem would be resolved. I then went to step one and followed the process. Yes, it was a complex problem, but if I had listened to what the Chief had said, I might not have conducted a test that proved the fault. When you come in to this kind of situation I encourage you to be better than I was. Politely listen, and then do it your way. They still failed. But you were nice…

When you get called in to un-fuck something, you can be sure that there are some very vested parties involved. Some might even want you to fail so they can say "I told you so". Stresses will be high and tempers short. You are going to have to navigate some treacherous territory in order for you to be able to do your job. Communication skills will be paramount. Building relationships -critical. Getting buy-in on your processes, helpful. You need to be viewed as an agent of positive change. We'll get into all of that, and more, later. For now, let's go back to the State Department and look at what *really* went wrong with the Visa Lottery.

Here's a surprise: When tested, the Electronic Visa Lottery Enrollment system worked. It was well designed. The problem actually derived from poor project management. In other words, it was a leadership failure. They didn't conduct a pilot program with real customers. The testing was done from consulates with high speed internet connections. There was no testing of whether or not the outreach communications were effective in reaching the intended customers. There was no consideration of how the changes would be handled by the customer. Wait. Scratch that last sentence. The State Department *did* consider the effects on customers. They sat around in conference rooms and talked to IT professionals, to consulate staff and to marketing specialists. What they did not do was ask the customer. They ran pilots in unrealistic environments then slapped each other on the back when they were successful.

In the world of Project Management there are Sponsors and Stakeholders. It's imperative that these individuals, groups or even systems are defined, then identified and their needs are understood and taken into consideration. Sponsors are typically the ones who are paying for the implementation. They can be stakeholders as well, and most often are. Stakeholders are those with a vested interest in the successful outcome. In our example, would you say the customers (applicants) are stakeholders? To my mind, they are the most important stakeholder. They will have the most at risk if the system fails to deliver. Other stakeholders would be the consulate, the systems and database administrators and anyone else who had risk, or a stake, in the implementation.

All of that is great and is the way a project or program should be set up. But this book isn't about how to set up a project. It's about how to fix a broken project. It's about how to identify where things went wrong and how to un-fuck it. As I have said from the beginning, to properly identify where things have gone wrong, you need to understand what they look like when things have gone right. So, where do you start?

"The only easy day was yesterday"

That's a Navy SEAL saying. I'm not sure it's a motto, but it could be. Let's face it. If fixing the problem was easy they wouldn't have called you in. How are you going to fill your customer (and your boss) with a sense of confidence that you are the right person to fix their problems? By the way, if they had only one problem, they wouldn't need you. Everything is fucked. So, no, it won't be easy.

You will instill your peers and your leadership with the confidence that you know what you are doing. You have a methodology, a process that you will use to help. You will actively listen to them and start to identify what the symptoms are. You won't jump to conclusions, even if you have already identified what you think is going on. You will listen to opinions, facts, and outright lies. You will write notes from every engagement, whether in a hallway, office or conference room. After the engagement you will put your notes into an email, bulletizing the specific points that are important to YOU. You will send this email to the parties involved, stating; "Here are the things we discussed today. Please review them and let me know if I got anything wrong or missed anything." You will save every single one of those emails forever. Trust me, they will come in handy. I recommend getting a read receipt if possible. This is called pro-active CYA. Covering Your Ass.

During my career I would say the most common issues that I was faced with would be called failed (or in dangerous risk) programs. Because I'm an IT guy, most things are IT related, but the process and the challenges will be similar across most business cases. The skills and methodologies I have learned come from personal experience, mentors, lessons learned from both successes and failures, and in some cases, good books. I've had a pretty diverse career. After over 16 years in the Navy, in 1997 I transitioned back to the civilian world. I was in the Washington, DC area and jobs for IT professionals were pretty easy to come by. For the next 20 years I would work as a government contractor. I worked for about a year as a systems engineer before getting hired to be the Network Manager for the Executive Office of the President of the United States. Next I was the IT Program Manager (PM) and acting chief engineer for the Office of Naval Research (ONR). Then, PM for the US Senate. Then PM at Unisys Corp., PM at the State Department, PM (Critical Infrastructure and Engineering; Risk Management) for the Office of the Secretary of Defense, followed by a role as

Director for a $16-billion program at NOAA. I worked for the Navy at Naval Sea Systems Command (NavSea) as an operations manager, and later, at the Explosive Ordinance Disposal Technical Division as a PM. Eventually, I ended up as a PM for the Office of the Inspector General at Homeland Security. It was there that I was able to make the jump to becoming a federal civilian employee at the Office of the Chief Technical Officer as Engineering Branch Chief and Deputy Director of the Technical Architecture and Engineering division.

I know that's a lot. Many people look at that and say I've held a lot of jobs, and that's true. As a government contractor this is pretty common. As someone who primarily comes in and puts out the fires and gets programs back to where they should be, my tenures were seldom over three years at one place. I spent 5 years at ONR.

The point is that I have had experience with a very diverse set of customer types. From our countries' President to NOAA to DHS and everything in between, each one was different in its own way. And yet, although the problems were different, each had similarities. The same processes that I used in one place worked at the next. Sure, there were unique challenges at each place. But the successes, and the failures, were all lessons learned. Each effort taught me something.

When you have used logic to examine a situation you will start using process of elimination to discover areas that could not be the cause of the symptoms. At its core, logical thinking is not thinking at all, it's reasoning. Thinking is a creative process that involves imagination and ruminations. What you want here is a scientific evaluation of the facts. Speaking of facts, don't trust them.

"Trust, but Verify"
- Ronald Reagan

Seriously, Gorbachev?

This was a lesson hard learned. When you come to a situation where things are screwed up and projects are in trouble, there will be a ridiculous amount of ass covering. Fingers will point everywhere. You are going to have to figure out who really wants to resolve things and who is just trying to keep their job by blaming others. It's okay to believe everything that you are told if you don't mind failing in your efforts. If you want to be successful, you'll verify what people set forth as facts.

It's time to get into the real nuts and bolts of the job of a Project Fixer. In the next chapters I'll talk about team building, personnel issues, creating relationships with leaders and customers, why a critical path is so important, communications management, handling accountability and delivering solutions.

CHAPTER 3

OWN IT

"Ownership is a commitment of the head, heart, and hands to fix the problem and never again fix the blame"
– John G. Miller

It is important to understand that your role as an UnFucker is to resolve problems. What it is not is to assign blame. That's a difference between you and everyone else. Because you have a methodology. When you discover the problems and start implementing changes, it will become evident where the mistakes were made. If leadership wants to do something about it, that's their role. Unless, of course, if it were members of your staff. Then you do what you must.

We covered steps 1, 2 & 3

1. Identify the problem. ...
2. Establish a theory of probable cause. ...
3. Test probable cause theory to determine actual cause. ...

Now let's look at 4, 5 & 6

4. Establish an action plan and execute the plan. ...
5. Verify full system functionality. ...
6. Document the process

When it comes to troubleshooting things like computers or cars, the six-step method works really great. But when you are dealing with more complex issues that include social matters and intermittent causes, things can get more difficult. Establishing a plan and then executing it sounds simple, but when you are troubleshooting people and orginizational issues, you may need to try many plans before you find what works. We'll talk about step 5 in detail when I address the 3M's. Step 6 is documentation. We cover this later when discussing Configuration and Change management as well as lessons learned. For now, let's dig into you, as a fixer.

We've talked about some of the basic ground rules to identify what's wrong. We examined the difference between symptoms and problems, the logical elimination of distractors (non-possible causes), and the importance of not depending on the skills of those who came before you (they failed to fix the problem).

You will have to own the issue if you are to be seen as the one who is going to fix the issue. Step up and proudly announce that you recognize that there is a problem. Clearly state that the system (form here on out, everything will be referred to as a system. Just remember it can be everything from relationships, devices, process; you get the point) is expected to perform in the manner that it was intended, and because it is not, it should be considered degraded or broken. Get consensus from the Sponsors and Stakeholders.

Getting consensus is important because if people don't admit there is a problem you will find it very difficult to get their support when you are trying to identify and resolve issues.

A friend of mine had a serious medical issue. The primary care doctor sent him to a specialist. The specialist said they think they know the problem. They called for a lot of lab tests, only to find themselves confused. So, they sent him to a different specialist, who said they think they know the problem. More lab tests created the same result. Another specialist and another…

When you start gathering information from your

stakeholders you may find that everyone you talk to seems to think the problem lies in their area of expertise. It's an ego thing. It's somewhat natural for you to take the first thing that you are told as gospel; to start running down the issues and to resolve the problem and be the hero. Resist the temptation and follow the process. You need to gather information from a majority of stakeholders before you can create a logical framework to support decision making and plan your attack for problem resolution.

You need to have buy-in from your sponsors. The ones who are paying you to be successful. They need to be informed of your findings and your proposed approach for next steps. You need their approval. You want to wrap them in the warm, fuzzy blanket of confidence that you know what you are doing and are following a logical path toward resolution. To do this, you don't point the finger of blame. You state the facts. Here's an example-

Initial findings regarding the implementation of the new portal website-
Goals:
- Create an external web interface for public access to documents, rules and regulations
- Use plain language
- Support accessibility
- Make downloads of document easy and available
- Provide real-time updates
- Maintain statistics of system use

Issues Identified:
- Many links to documents are not working
- Statistics do not appear to be accurate based on the number of failed downloads versus attempts
- Customer frustrations are leading to complaints

Next Steps:
- Evaluate the requirements for the repositories of

documents to be accessed by the public
- Review the requirements and parameters used in the gathering of statistics
- Evaluate customer feedback for consistency with the known issues. Use this data to determine if there are other unknown issues to be addressed

As you can see, this is a pretty basic documenting of activity. Note that no names are used. The fewer words used to get the point across, the better. This document will be either used to memorialize a discussion or to start one. What you are looking for here is official acceptance of the activities that you are going to undertake in your problem-solving methodology. If the things you are proposing are not accepted by your leadership, now is the time to find out. Not after expending time, resources, and energies in areas your sponsors don't agree with. Why? Because your approach might be wrong. In fact, there will be many times when it *is* wrong. Remember, if you are doing your job right, you created a list of probable problems. If there was only one possibility, you already finished your job, and everything is working as intended. But more likely is that there are many issues to be addressed and many things to be investigated. Most often, issues are a result of many unplanned events culminating in disaster. It isn't one problem that causes plane crashes; it's a chain reaction of a multitude of failures.

Semper Gumby

The motto of the Marine Corps is Semper Fidelis. Always Faithful. My motto is Semper Gumby; Always Flexible. If you don't know Gumby, look it up. If not, just trust me that it was a rubbery character from old cartoons. He had a horse named Pokey. Eddie Murphy did Gumby skits on Saturday Night Live. The point is he was flexible.

If you are going to be successful in this line of work, you had better be flexible. There is a big difference between being committed and being locked in. A person who is committed is both dedicated and open minded. A person who is locked in is so married to an idea or issue and cannot, even when the evidence says otherwise, accept they could be wrong. Dealing with these kinds of personalities is difficult. You won't be alone. Einstein had to deal with it when he introduced his theory of relativity.

Sometimes scientists have too much invested in the status quo to accept a new way of looking at things. This was certainly true when Albert Einstein's 1905 paper on "special relativity" first challenged the British conception of ether. Einstein argued that space and time were bound up together (something he would elaborate on in his theory of general relativity of 1915, adding gravity to the mix of space/time), a complicated idea that contradicted the long-held belief in something called ether. In the 19th century, ether (not to be confused with the once-popular anesthetic diethyl ether) was the medium that scientists believed filled space. It might be considered the first "dark matter," an undetectable something theory said should be out there, the explanation for a number of problems having to do with electricity, the movement of light, even the whole concept of "nothing." It was, according to one early-20th-century physicist, "accepted as a necessity by all modern physicists." But as Einstein's theory noted, there was no experimental confirmation for the substance. There was no proof it existed, other than that the scientific establishment had accepted the concept. As Stanley Goldberg reminds us, British physicists had a "theoretical commitment to the ether." For instance, Lord Kelvin argued in 1907 that ether must be an "elastic, compressible, non-gravitational solid." However, in the end it didn't conceptually work well enough.

– Matthew Wills, JSTOR Daily

People can, and will be, very married to their ideas and their ideology. They are invested in the truth of them. If their beliefs are proven wrong, how will they justify all the efforts they have invested? It will be hard to overcome these locked-in ideas. But being able, and more importantly, willing, to shift directions when the evidence supports it, is critical to be a successful fixer.

Another area where flexibility plays a strong role is in shifting requirements. In the PM world there is a thing called scope-creep. It's an occurrence that often begins as projects are being implemented. Maybe the requirements weren't defined well enough. Perhaps things changed, or new ideas were spawned because of the activities of the project implementation itself. Maybe a law changed, or a new security vulnerability was discovered.
Remember this from chapter 1?

If you can't tell me exactly what you want, I can't be sure I'm able to give it to you.

This is what that meant. Maybe your sponsors knew what they wanted when they started, maybe not. Maybe they changed their minds. Whatever the case, know that this is where most projects run into trouble. Here's another thought:

No plan survives first contact with the enemy.

No matter how well a project is thought out, once you begin implementation it is highly likely that you will discover things the you didn't expect. Remember Dr. Seuss's "How the Grinch Stole Christmas"? This is what I call my Cindy Lou Who story.

> December 2014: A British-born U.S. photojournalist and a South African aid worker held hostage in Yemen by al Qaeda militants have been 'murdered' in a failed rescue attempt. American citizen Luke

Somers had been held hostage since September 2013 in Yemen's capital Sana'a having moved to the country two years earlier. The 33-year-old was reportedly shot by his captors as Navy SEAL Team six, made up of around 40 men, carried out a dramatic rescue bid in the Wadi Abdan region of the southern Shabwa province late on Friday night. According to the Wall Street Journal, the commandos hiked for six miles through a mountain range to reach the village where he was being held. They were only 100 yards away from the compound when the terrorists reportedly heard a dog bark - prompting the militants to shoot the pair dead.

Two medics involved in the operation tried to revive both hostages, but one died at the scene while the other succumbed to his injuries on the operating table inside the USS Makin Island.

Why Cindy Lou Who? Because during the Grinch's late-night attempt to steal Christmas, he was surprised by little Cindy Lou Who. Unlike the SEAL's event with a barking dog, the Grinch was able to give her a glass of water and save his operation. How can you minimize the likelihood of high-impact issues ruining your best plans?

Think like a war planner.

CHAPTER 4

PLAN FOR FAILURE

This isn't what it sounds like. I'm not saying that you should plan to fail. What I'm saying here is that before you implement a project (also known as your solution to resolve issues with a project), you need to get a group of subject matter experts and stakeholders together and identify what could possibly go wrong. This is best done in a room with a big wall and a whole bunch of index card sized sticky notes.

You want to encourage out-of-the box thinking. Explain the Cindy Lou Who story or the SEAL example to illustrate the point. Then get people to start writing down their ideas of risks on their cards. Don't share yet. Ask everyone to put down at least five examples of possibilities. Challenge them to make at least one or two a far-fetched (but realistically possible) possibilities. Once everyone is done, start putting the sticky notes on the wall. You don't need to group them yet, just stick them up.

If you have more than a few people in this exercise, pick two or three and ask them to group the sticky notes. You shouldn't do this yourself. This is an opportunity for buy-in from your team. When they see themselves as part of your solution, you create a psychological commitment of their support for the agreed upon approach.

When you have everything put into groups, discuss the difference between likelihood and impact. In the table below, the left side represents the probability of the risk occurring. The bottom represents the impact caused if the risk occurred.

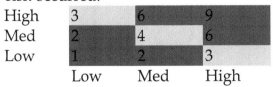

This tool gives you the ability to visualize where you need to focus your risk management efforts. Things in the red sector (those rated 6 and above; 3 and 4 are yellow; 1 and two are green) should certainly have a mitigation plan discussed. The rest needs to be decided by the team to determine if it is a risk that needs a plan or not. Some risks you simply accept. If you can't eliminate the risk, or if the elimination would be too costly, then you need to plan for failure.

What will you do if this risk manifests? You talked about it. You know it's possible. So have a plan. The plan might be to admit defeat and rollback. It might be to call upon expert third party support. Get the contact information first, reach out and share your intended activity and get advice. At minimum, have a contacts name and information documented so they can be called upon. You aren't planning to fail, you're planning on what action you will take if a risk happens.

"There are known knowns. These are things we know that we know. There are known unknowns. That is to say, there are things that we know we don't know. But there are also unknown unknowns. There are things we don't know we don't know."
-Donald Rumsfeld

You don't know what You don't know. So, in planning for risks, you also need a plan for what you will do if an unknown, unexpected event occurs. What would you do if during a computer system upgrade a lightning storm causes all the power to go out? Have a plan. And by the way, go back to chapter one and remember:

Importantly, before you take any action, if possible, make a backup copy of the system, so that you can

preserve everything as it is.

Every change to a system will have consequences. Hopefully, they will be the intended consequences. But sometimes things go wrong. That's why you should NEVER attempt a change without a fall back plan.

CHAPTER 5

NO MATTER WHERE YOU GO, THERE YOU ARE

For a problem to begin getting fixed, something must change. You need to embrace change. You need to be viewed as a driving force toward positive change. In fact, you are an Agent of Change.

In the world of IT Service Management there is something known as ITIL. ITIL is an acronym for Information Technology Infrastructure Library. ITIL concepts can really fit any business model. They don't have to be limited to only IT. The basic idea is that business services have a lifecycle. You start with a service strategy, then go outward to design, transition and then operation. Surrounding all of this is the concept and activities of continuous service improvement.

What I want to talk about here is Change Management. A leading cause of system failure is the lack of managed change. So many organizations are where they are now because of acting and reacting to things that either were not thought about or did not exist when they first implemented the system or organization. This results in an atmosphere where the original design is lost. New technologies were implemented. Security issues required patches; software upgrades were made. Departments were shifted, and new organizations formed. People, smart people, left and took their knowledge with them. The system now has no resemblance to the system design when it was originally conceived.

I've seen it everywhere I have worked. Without exception, at some level, every organization has had the same problem. They don't know where they are. Along with

Change Management is the big brother, Configuration Management. Again, these principals go across all fields. Think architecture, electrical schematics or even our own anatomy. We need to know where we are starting from before we can figure out how to get to where we want to be. In the first chapter, when discussing the six-step trouble shooting method, one of the considerations was "what changed?". The overwhelming majority of problems are caused by the unintended consequences of change. It may not reveal itself immediately. It may cause a chain of events before it is manifested, but rest assured, somewhere, somebody or something changed and created the issue. Something got F'd. Good thing you're here.

In the perfect world, everything is written down. The original diagram of all systems. How they interact with other systems, both internal to the organization, and external. This diagram creates a baseline configuration. The place from which all deviations are started. If you were to look at a map and say you wanted to go to San Francisco, the baseline configuration would be to know where you are starting from. Would your path be different if you started from New York or Alaska? Of course. You have to know where you are to make an effective plan to get to where you want to be.

Bad news. We don't live in a perfect world. Good news- because of that, we need people like you to Un-F*ck stuff. Never get angry at the people who screw all this stuff up. If nobody made mistakes, you'd have to find a different line of work. I'm thankful for all the dummies of the world. I love them.

You're going to have to deal with the likelihood that often you won't know what the baseline configuration of a system is when you first come into a situation.

A few words of advice here: Most senior leaders know that this is an issue. It will be tempting for you to complain about the lack of basic engineering and business best practices. If you decide to go down this path, expect your tenure to be short. People don't want you to tell them what they already know. They want you to fix it. The lack of a well-managed configuration baseline and change control will almost always be part of the root cause to problems. It is seldom the resolution to the problem at hand. When the time comes for recommendations on how to reduce future problems, you can introduce the idea of re-baselining the system configuration and implementing a, strong change management plan.

Now that you fixed the problem and the system is working as expected, you have the prime opportunity to document (Step 6) the system in its static state. This is how it looks when it works. Take a picture (figuratively) and make sure it gets implemented into a change control program.

But wait- we still need to figure out what's wrong with the situation at hand- a poorly (or non-existent) documented system.

Reverse Engineering; err...starting from the end

In many cases, you are under time constraints. As the leader of the effort to get everything working as designed, you will have Resources (budget, personnel, equipment), Scope (specific requirements on the definition of success, sometimes called deliverables) and Time. These three things make up the Project Management Triad; Scope, Resources, and Time. Often referred to as the 3 constraints of project management, Scope, Time and Cost (I use resources here to be more specific) are how you should manage your efforts.

Each report that you present to your sponsor should include an assessment of these constraints. Your original review and identification of The Problem is one project. Once you have identified The Problem (or possible probable problems) you need to create a separate proposal on how you will approach resolving the issue. This is important because you may not be called upon to conduct the resolution. Know the meaning of "Done" before taking on the work.

Your sponsor will be juggling many responsibilities. They often have shifting priorities and fixed budgets. They may need to shift resources from your efforts to other duties. You need to be able to represent the impact to your project so that they can make informed decisions. Where you take away from one part of the triad, you must add to another. If you reduce my staff, it will take more time. If you add to the scope of work to be performed but don't add more time, I'm going to need more staff. If your sponsor understands the impact to your project, they might decide to look somewhere else for their shifting needs. If you do have to change your plan, be sure to memorialize the decision in an email that documents the old plan, the changes required, the impact, and the new plan scope/time/cost. CYA.

When you have a hard, fixed deadline, a good approach to managing to the deadline is to start at the end, where you want to be, and work your way back to where you are. You can do this by creating an Integrated Master Schedule, and then define the Critical Path. The Integrated Master Schedule (IMS) is a time-based schedule containing the networked, detailed tasks necessary to ensure successful program/contract execution. The primary purpose of an IMS is to provide all project participants with a consistent tool for planning, executing and tracking technical, schedule, cost and risk activity. Now that you know where you want to be and where you are, you need to define your path. The *how* to get there.

Critical Path: Follow the Yellow Brick Road...

There are books on this subject. Most of them are good. You can read them if you want. What is important here is a much more simplified approach. As an Agent of Change, you need to manage to the critical path. Why? Because you are a leader. You don't know everything. You can't do all the activities. You should NOT be "hands-on". What you should be-strike that- what you *must* be, is informed. Knowledgeable. Responsible.

If you have done your job right, you will have brought together a team (more discussion on that later) who are skilled professionals in the areas needed to implement your problem resolution plan. They will have played a large part in the creation of the plan and given you information about the effort and time involved in the implementation. They will execute the plan. Not you. You are the General, The Captain of the Ship, the Coach of the team. If they fail, you will get fired, not them.

Have you ever heard of the Manhattan Project? During WWII, from 1942 to 1946, it was the code name for a project to develop the first nuclear weapons. The scope was well defined- develop a nuke- and the cost was pretty much unlimited (about $25 billion in today's dollars). But the Time- that was critical. Each day spent in development meant more allied forces and civilian lives lost. This is one of the first recorded uses of the Critical Path method of project management.

There were hundreds of things to do. Hundreds of people involved. Many of the same resources were needed for many different tasks. Many tasks couldn't be started until others were completed. They were dependent.

If you imagined a project timeline that was linear, it would probably start on the left with Day 1 and end somewhere on the right with the Final Day. Everywhere in between would be all the activities that were required to be finished on the Final Day. But guess what. You don't care. What, you say? I said; "You don't care".

All those tasks are not important to you. You hired or have appointed staff that need to care about those tasks.

They are professionals in their fields; subject matter experts. Trust them to do their jobs.

I want to be unique, just like everybody else.

I get it. You want to be special. It's okay, you are. But in order for you to focus on the bigger picture, you need to let other special people focus on the details. If you spend all of your time managing the details you will burn out, make your team think you don't have faith in them and be unavailable to focus your energies where needed more. What you need is to define, understand, and manage to, the critical path.

In most cases, I will depend on my team leads to define the critical path. When they do it, it's hard for them to say the tasks are unachievable. You are going to hold them accountable for the activities that are required to complete that gate on the critical path.

In the basic terms, you need to map out the most important tasks in the project and use that to estimate the duration required to complete the project. To expand on this, you might want to get your team together and talk about what needs to be accomplished to reach that specific goal.

Let's pretend you have the project of building a car. This is, of course, being simplified for illustrative purposes. I have no idea how to build a car. But I brought together a team of people who do know how. Tell them that you are looking to block diagram as much as possible here. Don't use minutia like all the activities that go into building the transmission- just installing a transmission; what you want here is the fact that the transmission must be installed. We're not discounting that the transmission needs to be built, but you have a team of experts for that. You don't need to know how they do it. You need to know that it gets done. What activities can't be started until the transmission is installed? These things would go to the right of the Transmission on your timeline. For example, you can't install the drive train or put the body on the chassis until the transmission is in place. This makes the block INSTALL TRANSMISSION a dependency on your critical path. This is what you want to manage.

You will ask your team of professionals to estimate the time (duration, not date) that it will take to get the transmission ready to install. You will determine if the team has any dependencies before they can get to work on the transmission job. Those dependencies would go to the left of INSTALL TRANSMISSION block on you project plan timeline.

Some activities can be taking place at the same time the transmission is being built. We could be putting on wheels, building the body, whatever. The point is our timeline is not entirely focused on completing one task before we move to the next. Work can be done concurrently, provided the staff and skillsets (resources) are not working on other tasks. It is therefore possible that a resource may be a dependency on a task completion.

The below is from workamajig.com-

Every project, regardless of its size or budget, has some core tasks that are crucial to its completion.
Take something as simple as making an omelet.
If you had to create a short recipe for making an omelet, it would look something like this:
- *Beat 2 eggs*
- *Heat a pan, add butter/oil when hot*
- *Pour in the beaten eggs and cook for 5 minutes*

There are several other tasks you need to perform to make a good omelet. You have to season the eggs with salt and pepper. Maybe add some vegetables and some cheese. Perhaps you could flip it on the other side so the eggs are fully cooked through.
However, these activities are in-addition to the three core steps in the recipe. Even if you don't perform them, you'll still have an

omelet. Not a very good one, but an omelet nonetheless.
On the other hand, if you forget to beat the eggs, or heat the pan, or cook the eggs, you won't have anything but a cold pan and two eggs.
Which is to say, the three steps in the recipe describe the critical tasks necessary to make the omelet making project a success.

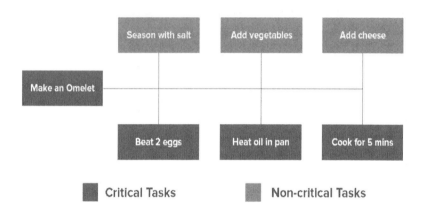

And the sequence of these steps describes the **critical path** a new cook must take if he wants to make an omelet.
Here is a sample of a much more complex critical path diagram:

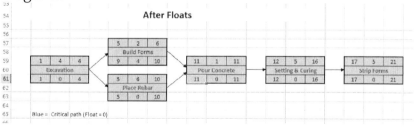

In this example, build forms and place rebar are concurrent tasks. As the manager, you don't need to know how to mix concrete. You don't need to know how to operate the excavator. What you need to know is that the job was completed on time and the dependent activities are now ready to begin.

The point to this entire discussion is that you need to understand the steps that are required to complete the entire project, but you need to manage to the critical path. When you report to your sponsor, you might choose to define these steps along the critical path as "gates". You should list the gate that is in progress with the estimated completion date and the next gate in the process. Each gate must have an identified responsible party. That person needs to understand and accept their role as Gatekeeper. It is the Gatekeeper, and only the Gatekeeper, that you will get information about the task from. This could be a team leader or SME, but you want to have someone knowledgeable on the task at hand. They are going to give you the projected completion date. You are going to hold them to it.

You will explain to the Gatekeeper that this is their gate, and you trust them to make sure that all of the minute tasks that need to be completed get done. Moreover, the Gatekeeper is responsible to inform you of any roadblocks to the successful and timely completion of the total critical path task. There are dependencies to be concerned with and any effect to the timeline will create ripples down the line.

When I talk about managing to the path, I mean that you hold your staff accountable to their projections.

A few paragraphs back I said you want to define duration of tasks, not dates. It is more important for you to understand how long it will take for a task to be completed than it is to know what date it will be done. Timelines should be created showing numbers of days to achieve the goal because it makes it much easier to be, well, Semper Gumby. When you set a date, people's minds get firm and fixed on that date. If something happens that you don't hit that date, you're seen as a failure. Dates may be required for the end of a project or for places along the critical path, but if an individual or even a group of tasks don't get completed exactly as expected, you might still be able to catch up elsewhere. No need to cause panic with stakeholders or the sponsor if it isn't necessary.

CHAPTER 6

HOW DOES AN ANT EAT AN ELEPHANT?

Resolving programmatic problems is complicated. If it was a simple task, you wouldn't be needed. The more challenging the issue, the better. As stated earlier, you are likely to be facing a multitude of issues that culminates to create the problem. In many cases the problem could have been solved early on, when it was simple. But, it was ignored or not considered to be a real issue. It could be personality, skillsets, work product errors, staffing, you name it. You will probably find it's a combination of several factors. When you first look at things, it might be really overwhelming. Somewhere in Africa lies the dead body of an elephant. The ant looks at this as an overwhelming task. But then...

He takes the first bite. And that is the answer to the question "how does an ant eat an elephant?". One bite at a time. The reason that we break a program down into a critical path is that it allows you to see the whole program as a group of individual bites. On their own, they might not be hugely significant, but when taken on the whole, they complete the project.

In the next few sections I will be talking about leadership and the management of programs from the perspective of accomplishment. The concepts of how to get things done. What to do when you have inherited a broken team. How to deal with negativity, disruptions and people who simply want you or your program to fail.

So, where do you start? Let's suppose that you start at the very beginning. You need a resume so that you can get an interview so that you can get a job so that you can fix the problem(s) and get paid.

How should your resume look to get attention and land the interview? Well, that's the first thing to understand. The resume isn't going to get you hired. It's going to get you the interview. So, it should be focused to do that single task.

There are a lot of books on writing resumes. Most are crap. They are out of date and have little to no relevance to the type of work that you do. Here are my suggestions.

1. Be professional in everything, from your email address to your formatting style. If your email is "SexyDude754", don't put that on a resume. Change it to something more professional. It might even be good to have an email address dedicated to your resumes. Pick one font type for your entire resume. The easier it is to read, the better. Use either Times New Roman, Arial, or Courier. The smallest size allowed is 10, largest is 14.
2. Your name and contact info are all you need for the top. No address. One phone number and one email. Nothing else. Your address is just taking up valuable space, and employers aren't supposed to ask where you live, so why volunteer the details?
3. In the first three to five sentences, you will detail
   a. First - State the position you want to be hired for. If you want a position as a Program Manager, say so. If you want a position as a Director of Operations, say so. Don't make the employer guess.
   b. Second - State what general qualities you would bring to the position
   c. Third - Why you want the position.
   d. If you needed a couple extra sentences to get your point across, fine. Just don't go over five.
4. Make sure that the employment experience is relative to the job you are seeking. You don't need to tell

about your time at Burger King. Don't go any further than the past 10 years or five positions, whichever comes first. The details you include should not be a list of duties and responsibilities that you had. Instead, it should be a list of things you did that made you a valuable employee. Think about data here; Did you save money, increase profit, streamline a system, improve processes? Give dollar values, percentages or some metric that will give your prospective employer information about how you might be a valuable resource to them.

5. Same for awards or accomplishments. Your resume doesn't need to talk about your hobbies or if you finished a marathon. But if an award is relevant to the position you are seeking, include it.
6. Your listed education should be post-high school and any job-related additional training or certificates you hold. If you do not have a college education, put your high school details.
7. The minimum length of a resume is 2 pages. The maximum is 4. Don't write a novel; write enough to get the interview.
8. No need for references. You can do that after the interview.
9. At the end of your resume, ASK FOR AN IN-PERSON INTERVIEW!!

After you have written your resume you should think about some things. Did you use key words that will get your resume flagged on a job search engine? Is it concise and to the point? Are there unnecessary words or flowery language? Add key words where it makes sense. Make sure the resume is simplistic enough for a screener to understand it. Realize that the screener who will decide if your resume moves forward is unlikely to have much of a clue about your job. They will just be looking for key words. Make it simple for them to select your resume.

Okay, so let's jump ahead. You nailed the interview and got the job. What are the first steps that you need to take? You are going to be introduced to a lot of people. You might be inheriting a team, or you might need to build a new one. But first things first. You need to learn about...

Your Boss, Your Customer and Who Pays You...

They might be all the same. In most cases, they are not. If you do contract work, you might have a "company boss" and a "customer boss". You may get a check from your company, but don't lose sight of the fact that the customer is the source of that pay. Contracting companies might want you to think that they are your boss, but when it comes down to it, if you don't keep your client happy, you won't keep your job.

Your first challenge will be to get the lay of the land and manage the perception of your clients toward you. You should be in listen mode. Remember, you got the job based on your qualifications and experiences and the expectation that you are the right person to solve the problems. Be cautious of your appearance. You are a professional. Dress like it. If the environment that you will be working in is more casual, adjust as needed, but always dress as good as your customer boss.

When you are in meetings, be sure to stay in listen mode, even if you have some important input. For now, unless you are asked, hold your ideas close. You are in those meetings because you belong there. You don't need to seek approval or show how smart you are. They already know that, or you wouldn't be there.

What you are trying to identify here are key players. You should be learning the different sponsors and stakeholders in your program. You need to figure out who the customers are. You're going to ask these people, outside of meetings, what challenges there are with respects to your program. You don't want to ask these questions in the group meetings. Some people will feel like you are calling them out. Some people won't be forthright because of the audience. In most cases, you will get a more sincere and complete response in a one-on-one discussion.

I know I mentioned it before, but this is another time when you memorialize your conversations. Make sure to write a follow-up email to the individual and state the pertaining discussion points and your understanding. Give them the opportunity to correct any areas if you got something wrong. Save these emails. It's going to help you develop your plan.

You're going to want to have a regularly scheduled meeting with your client boss. Hopefully, this person is also the project sponsor. If not, that's okay. Just be sure that you are talking to the person accountable for the success of the program. You are going to want to share the names of the people that you have talked to and verify if you have talked to everyone that you should have. Note that you didn't ask first who you should talk to- you are showing that you are proactive and take initiative. Next, you will discuss the general areas of challenges and concerns that you found during your discovery interviews. Don't attribute the specific comments to the people who made the comments. This is not about placing blame. It is never your position to place blame. This is about defining symptoms and possible probable problems.

As part of your discussion, you should be trying to test the level of agreement with your discoveries. Does your client believe that you are on the right track? Do they challenge some of the assessments? Do they have ideas or areas where they think you might focus to find more or other challenges?

After this discussion (memorialized with email, of course), you are going to start putting together an initial project review. You want to be able to state, specifically, the goal of the project by defining what the expected goal is. Note that it may have changed when first begun. You want to state the goal as of today. The second part of the report will be to define where the project is. What has been done? What is still required? You need to get commitment, acceptance and agreement from the stakeholders that you know what the definition of success is and what proof will be required. You need everyone to agree that you have defined all the issues known at that time. If they don't agree, find out what they would add and come up with logic-based acceptance or denial. Every issue must be a logical possible contributor to the defined shortfalls. This will help you to define your critical path.

It's time to talk about some challenges that you might (probably) be faced with in the wonderful world of inner-office politics. You are going to be faced with many different personalities in various positions of authority. Some will view you as a positive agent of change. Some will view you as a disrupter, causing them more work. Some people might even view you as a challenge to their position in the organization. You need to be able to identify all of them for what they are. You need to identify who is most important to the successful implementation of your plan. You do not have to be everyone's friend, but you need be no one's enemy.

If you were successful in defining and getting agreement on the challenges, you at least got verbal commitment from the important people to the program. The commitment might not be what is in their heart, but what is important is that you got it on record. And your follow-up email gave everyone the opportunity to change their mind or "correct the record".

Understanding the personal motivations of the leaders you will be working with will make your job easier. What motivates people to do things? How will their effort (that you need) benefit them? Humans are not that complex when

it comes to motivation. We all have basic needs. They are:
- Security; Live & Be Healthy.
- Variety; Opportunity; not feel trapped.
- To love and be loved.
- Contribution and Creation; to be a part of something
- Esteem and Identity; to feel important; valued.
- Self-governance (Autonomy) and Freedom.
- Significance and purpose.

So, what motivates you? It may be one, some or even all these things. If you can determine what it is that motivates the people you are working with, you can play to their wants, needs and motivations in your daily interactions. Just be sincere about it. Are they a football fan? Are they buying a new house? Do they hate their job because they feel trapped? Be empathetic to their situations. Understand that you are not going to solve any of their issues or buy a house for them but show interest and find ways to be seen as value added in the relationship. If you don't have an interest in the things they are passionate about, at least be a good listener. Empathy shares with frustrations and shows understanding. You don't need to validate and agree with them, but you do have to show that you understand them. Often you only need to say; "Wow, that seems rough. I've known others who felt that way and they had a tough time. Let me know if I can help some way". Other times you may have had similar experiences and can share. Just be careful not to upstage them or simplify their issue. To them, it's important.

There are different personality types to deal with too. Particularly for those in leadership roles.

Ever heard of the Myers Briggs Personality type test? Some know it as the MBTI.

"Explore your personality type with our assessment, based on the original 16 personality types created by Isabel Briggs Myers and Carl Jung. Discover how to choose your optimal career path,

unlock your potential and develop more fulfilling relationships!"

About 1.5 million people take the test online each year, and more than 88% of Fortune 500 companies, as well as hundreds of universities, use it in hiring and training, according to The Myers Briggs Company, a California-based firm that administers the MBTI. Even fictional characters, from Disney princesses, to Harry Potter and Darth Vader have been assigned an MBTI type.

The MBTI was invented in 1942 by Katharine Cook Briggs and her daughter, Isabel Briggs Myers. Cook, always a keen observer of people and their differences, was inspired by the work of psychologist Carl Jung and his theories; for example, the concepts of introversion and extroversion. The mother and daughter devoted their lives to developing the type indicator, hoping to help people understand their tendencies and choose appropriate jobs. The test uses 93 questions to assess the following traits:

- Introvert (I) versus Extrovert (E)
- Intuitive (N) versus Sensory (S)
- Thinking (T) versus Feeling (F)
- Judging (J) versus Perceiving (P)

Based on the combination of traits people fall into, the test ultimately assigns them one amongst the sixteen labels, like INTJ, ENFP, and so on.

Here's the problem. It's bogus.

You are either an extrovert or introvert, a judger or a feeler. Can't you judge *and* be empathetic? Can you be introverted about somethings and extroverted about others?

My feelings are that a test developed in the 1940's may not have grown with us over the years. But there is value in this kind of effort. You can learn a lot about people and what they think of themselves with a test like this. I tend to base my assessments of people and their personalities more on observation and experiences. It is the personality of the moment that you have to work with. Let's examine some leadership personalities.

- **Positive and Negative -Leaders or Bosses?**

    These either motivate by award, recognition or frequent pats on the back. These are leaders. Bosses criticize, downplay success by saying; "so what, you did your job!". A good thing to look for here is to praise in public but criticize only in private.

- **Authoritarian leadership**.

    An autocratic leader centralizes power and decision-making in himself. He gives orders, assigns tasks and duties without consulting the employees. They full authority and should assume full responsibility. This style is negative, based on threats and punishment. Subordinates act as he directs. He doesn't care about staff opinions. He believes that because of his authority he alone can decide what is best in a given situation.

    *see Helicopter story below.

- **Democratic leadership**.

    Also known as consensus leadership, this type of leader gets buy-in from the staff. They feel involved in decision making and valued as members of a team. This typically results in increased cooperation with management, higher motivation, reduction of grievances and less absenteeism and employee turnover.

- **The Laissez-faire leadership**.

    The laissez-faire or non-interfering type of leader passes on the responsibility for decision-making to his subordinates and takes a minimum of initiative in administration. He gives no direction and allows the group to establish its own goals and work out its own problems. This is a common style of people who are just waiting on retirement. Please, I don't want to be responsible for anything. I'll blame it on my team...

- **Paternalistic leadership**.

Paternalism means father knows best. It's the same relationship between the head of the family and the members of the family. The leader guides and protects his subordinates as members of his family. As the father figure, he provides his subordinates with good working conditions and fringe benefits. It is assumed that workers will work harder out of gratitude.

In today's age, most people need a combination of styles to be happy at work. You need to be able to recognize these styles, so you can understand how each leader views themselves and how their staff views their leader. You're going to need more than just cooperation; you need to show how their activity and involvement will result in value to them, both on a business and a personal level.

A Helicopter Story

In the early nineties, heading up to the whole Somalia and Blackhawk Down era, I was stationed aboard an LHD (Amphibious Carrier, basically). We had a contingent of Marines and sailors that supported A/V 8B Harrier jump jets and an array of different types of helicopters. The division I was in took care of the NATO Sea Sparrow missile systems. Our Division Officer, however, was a young Lieutenant (Junior Grade) and a helicopter pilot. I don't know why he was doing a tour as our DivO, but it didn't matter. He was the boss.

We were in port, getting all the systems ready for the constant inspections and pre-deployment activities you have to go through. Everyone had work to do and it was a busy time. When it came time for liberty everyone who wasn't on duty went ashore for R&R or family time. One of the junior enlisted, Seaman Smurf, we'll call him, always seemed to bust his ass but was constantly getting dinged for one small thing or another. He had a lot on his mind. As a just-married E-2, his pay wasn't much more than the minimum to get by on. The last time he went home on leave he had intended on bringing his wife back to Norfolk with him to live off base. It would be tight, but they could make it.

Then he found out the ship was getting ready to deploy on a six-month cruise. So, they decided she would stay home in Indiana where she had a support network of family and friends. On the night before he was to return to the ship, she gave him the news. She took the test that morning. They were going to have a baby.

The proud Dad-To-Be was treated to toasts for the next few hours. When he awoke, he was late for his plane trip and ended up late for duty. In the Navy, we call it UA, or unauthorized absence. You might know it better as AWOL.

The division Chief Petty Officer (CPO) listened to his story and decided to go easy on him. It was his first real offense, and he was a hard worker, although not the best. Over the next six months sea deployment, Seaman Smurf got into one minor thing after another. Nothing was ever major, but the DivO clearly had it out for the kid. The deployment was hard. No real ports of call near Somalia and not much time to visit anyway. We were at operational tempo for the majority of time, so I can safely say that it wasn't fun time.

When we returned to port we had some stand down time. Seaman Smurf came to the CPO with a terrible look of concern. His wife was in trouble and the doctors were going to induce labor in three days. "Please, Chief- I need to take unscheduled leave to be with my wife and see my baby born". The chief told him to fill out the request and walk it through his section leader, then to the chief and then to the DivO. "Aye, aye". Off he went.

Several hours later he came back to his Chief out on

deck. Something was very wrong. Smurf could barely breathe, he was so upset. Chief told him to get a grip, suck it up and tell him what his major malfunction was. Smurf proceeded to explain how the Division Officer tore him a new one. Wanted to know why he should do any favors for him, a fuck up. There were plenty of people who should be allowed to take leave before him. Smurf tried to explain the situation but only got more grief. You should have thought about that before you came back to the ship UA the last time!

Chief had heard enough. He told Smurf to lay below to his division's berthing spaces and he'd come down to see him in a while. Then the Chief went to the DivO's office. He reminded the young officer that, as a Navy Chief Petty Officer, it was part of his duty and responsibility to aid and mentor junior officers. So, he said, sitting on the DivO's desk, "Listen".

"There are events that can make or break your career. Sometimes young leaders act like a puppy in a forest. They think they have to piss on every tree to mark their territory, show who's boss. Then there's the ones who think leading through intimidation will get you the best followers. But you have to know who is working for you. You're a Lt(jg), ready for promotion to full Lieutenant. Smurf is a damn E-2 (Private in the army). If you deny him liberty to see his baby born, he'll probably go anyway. What's the worst you can do? Bust him a paygrade back to E-1? What's that going to cost him? Probably less than $100 a month.

"On the other hand, if you tell him how hard it was to make this decision, how you are considering his wife and family above his needs- tell him that, with another mouth to feed, he's going to need to get promoted. Tell him he's going to need your support and then sign the damn leave papers. When Smurf comes back, he'll be devoted and appreciated to you. And he will tell his shipmates how you had his back when it was so important.

"Or, one day, you can be getting in your 5-million-dollar helicopter, going over your safety checklist, heading out into a war situation. When you look down and see Seaman Smurf's name on the maintenance list. Who held a grudge. Or not, but you won't know, will you?"

Smurf went on leave. And he was grateful. He named his son after the Chief. At least that's what he told me. His wife said he was named after her father, who just happened to be another Robert.

When you are a leader of people, in order to get the most out of them, you need to know them. You need to take an interest in their lives both in and out of the office. That doesn't mean you have to go drinking with them or bowling or whatever. It means you need to know something about their passions and what drives them.

When you have defined the critical path, you are going to have to determine who the mid-level leaders need to be. The Gatekeepers. Not who they are right now, but who they need to be for this project.

I want to go back for a moment to talk more about items on the critical path and how to manage to them. When you have your critical path all drawn out, and everyone has agreed that it is correct, you need to consider the resources required to complete the tasks. You will assign a gatekeeper to each critical path dependency gate (only one per gate, though). One person may be the Gatekeeper on more than one gate.

You are not going to eat the entire elephant in one bite. You are going to look to the very first gate on your path. You are going to have your Gatekeeper report to you on what resources they need and how much time that it will take to complete the task. You make sure they understand that you are holding them responsible to their own plan. You are not going to bug them. You hired highly skilled professionals and you know they will get the job done. You will require a periodic report (you decide, I usually do weekly) to declare if there are any challenges that you might be able to help with. If there is a roadblock, you are to be notified immediately.

While this work is being completed, you need to be looking at the next gate. How can you ease the way to completion? Consider the resources that will be required. Make sure they will be available to perform the duties as needed. Be support to your Gatekeeper.

Reporting things has become a pet peeve of mine over the past few years. I'm tired of being told a job is 80% complete after two weeks, but it's 3 more weeks before its 100% complete. I have decided that I don't want to know that data anymore. I want to know it's done or it is not done. If it's not done, is it on schedule? I don't want to know the details. If you are going to make the Gate, that's awesome. I expected you would. If not, you need to bring me details on what your blockers are and how it will impact the expected timeline.

CHAPTER 7

NERDS, GEEKS, THE ARTSY-FARTSY TYPES AND MILLENNIALS

If you were to read management books written in the 70s, 80's or even the 90's, you would find that most of them viewed employees as if everyone was a factory worker. Every employee was the same. Not to denigrate factory workers, but our society has changed. Back then, the Manager was probably the only one who was college educated. They might have been the smartest person in the room. Today, I would challenge that. I surround myself with people who are smarter than I am every chance I get. Why? Because, as a leader, I know it's not about me. It's about the job.

Getting the job done requires the right skill sets to be applied to the right activities. Being a leader is like conducting an orchestra. You need different people with differing talents to make the best music. You might be one hell of a trombone player. Good for you. But you need violins, too for a great symphony.

Diversity is a good thing. When I talk about diversity, I don't mean ethnicity or orientation exclusively. I mean culture, background, training, experiences and viewpoints. The nerds and geeks of today are unbelievably talented engineers, designers and developers. The artsy-fartsy crowd are the creative backbone for social media, graphic arts and idea factories. The Millennials bring a fresh perspective on the motivations of the soon-to-be largest consumer block around. By bringing a team together with a diverse set of skills and viewpoints, you create the ability to see things in a way you never would have if left to your own. But how do you manage such a group? One size does not fit all.

Work Product: Show me the Money!

In the movie "Jerry McGuire", where Tom Cruise played a sports agent, Cuba Gooding, Jr. had the role of the football player Tom Cruise represented. His mantra; "Show me the Money!" became a famous movie quote for trivia fans. He didn't care about the hard work his agent was doing. He didn't care about who he was going to play for. All he cared about was the Money. In our view, the money is the work product.

There are many different definitions for work product, but for our purposes, go with this: Work product is the tangible results of efforts that are required parts to achieve a goal. If you apply this to a gate on a critical path, you will be able to view work product as a list of activities that must be completed before the "gate" can be defined as done. You should require your Gatekeeper to have the list of work products required and to share them publicly with the people who are tasked with the completion.

When you get a report on the progress, it should go something like this: "For Gate 3, Customer Acceptance Testing, we have completed 6 of 23 work products. We anticipate completing 5 more by the next reporting date. We do not have any roadblocks identified and expect to complete the Gate as scheduled."

Notice that this was not a discussion. It's a report. It provides you, the leader, with all the information you require. Many people will want to tell you about all the wonderful things they did, the challenges that they overcame and yada, yada, yada. You can certainly listen, but really, you don't care. What you care about is that the activity is happening and the Gatekeeper doesn't need your help for anything. In other words, Show me the Money. The other stuff is just fluff.

On the other hand, what if there are roadblocks? Then what? Your Gatekeeper must report to you the same information but include what the roadblock is, what activity is required to overcome the roadblock, and when that activity will occur. If they need outside assistance (external to their own resources), who do they need? How will this roadblock effect the timeline associated with completion of the Gate? With this information in hand, you will bring to bear all of the forces needed to either resolve the roadblock or create a workaround (detour). You will also inform your sponsor of any effect that will be had on the timeline. If there is none, you don't need to inform the sponsor. They won't care. Unless, of course, your sponsor is part of the roadblock resolution.

As we are likely to adopt existing teams of resources we will have to adopt the personalities as well. Your Gatekeepers aren't going to be managers. They will more likely be experts in a particular work product area. That means you are going to have to provide the management skills for the staff supporting the total effort. These skills will include communications, conflict resolution, some human resource activities, and performance management. Out of all of these, communication is the most important.

Earlier, I said that almost every program in trouble will have, at its root, an issue with configuration management. Now, I will tell you that communication is a leading contributor to most, if not all, failing programs. Therefore, it makes sense that the first thing you should work on is developing and acting on a communications plan.

In the world of Project Management, there is a document referred to as a communication plan. These are normally well thought out and inclusive as a deliverable near the beginning of the project start date. In so many cases, they are not read by the customer. They are not read by the project staff. They are not followed in any appreciable way. So why have them? If you are fortunate enough to be on a project that uses the communications plan, and it is a good one, it's unlikely the project would be failing. Possible, but not common.

As the fixer, you need to fix the communications issues. You might want to see the plan, but it's not necessary. You really need to create a plan of your own that suits your purposes. Focused on the problem resolution, your plan will be targeted at your sponsor and stakeholders, subject matter experts and Gatekeepers, and the customer. But what should the plan include?

1. What do you want people to know?
2. Who do you want to know it?
3. How do you want the information to get to them?
4. What format should the communication be in?
5. When, and how often, do you need the communication to go out?

There are different types of information. There's need to know, nice to know, and the other stuff. You want to focus on the need to know things. Why? Because you are focused on a job. When your communications are focused, the conversations that it evokes will tend to stay within that focus. You want to think about not only what you are saying, but how you will be heard. Whether you are communicating in a report or in a discussion, you need to remain aware of the difference between what you say and what people hear. Does that make sense?

I asked, "Does that make sense?" because this is a phrase you can use to gage the depth of understanding people have of what you have said. It gives them an opportunity to seek clarification. Watch body language and expressions. Some people won't raise a question even if they don't really follow what you are saying. If you are communicating in writing, always remember to ask if there are questions or concerns and request feedback.

Not everyone needs to have all the information, all the time. Be sure to define who the appropriate audience is for the information that you are sharing. It's a good idea to ask if there is anyone not included (missed) that this information would be valuable to. You should define groups and create a chart of which groups get which type of communications.

Information can come in many forms. Reports, white papers, studies, surveys, etc. Meetings, conferences and phone calls are also communications. Numbers 3 and 4 above are about the method that you will share the information. The prime purpose for all of this activity is to Trust but Verify that your communications have not only occurred but were received and understood. You don't want anyone to be able to say, "Nobody told me!".

On your chart you created showing the groups and types of communications, you need to add the periodicity. This can easily be incorporated into off or online calendar events as a reminder to you, or perhaps you print out the chart and keep it in your line of sight. You may need to gather information from others to create reports, so be sure to give yourself enough time to collect data.

By actively communicating with your sponsors, stakeholders, customer and staff, you are creating an environment where people will need to rise to your level of professionalism. By doing your job right, you will soon see that senior leaders will start encouraging the rest of their teams to follow your example. Yea, you. Keep in mind that the way you communicate to a room full of engineers may be far different from the way you speak to a group of executives. Know your audience.

Another Meeting? Seriously???

Okay, I'll say it. Meetings suck. They are time wasting opportunities for egocentric, self-focused people to say, "look at me, I'm important". Alright. Now that that's out of the way, you can entertain yourself by the couple hundred thousand memes about meetings available on the Internet. I'll wait.

You back? Cool. Meetings can be important opportunities to communicate, learn and get buy-in. The reason that most people see meetings as one of the many levels of hell is that people have never been taught *how* to have a meeting. Most meeting invites will say something like:
When: Tuesday, March 4, 9am to 10am
Where: Conference Room 4
Subject: Project Z

This invitation is the first sign that you're going to a time-suck. How can you prepare for this? Who is going to be there and why?
A better invite has the information listed above, but also includes:
Agenda: Review project schedule and completed activities; report on upcoming activities and deliverable dates; Identify any roadblocks and mitigation strategies
Goal: Ensure all stakeholders are aware of current status and any challenges

This is much better because it lets people prepare for the discussion. They can anticipate what questions they might be asked and come ready to answer. It also provides a purpose. This enables the meeting host to keep things focused on the subject at hand. If a topic comes up that is important and warrants discussion, table it and get back on track. The best part- If you reach the goal of the meeting before the allotted time, you're done. Go back to what you were working on. I know this sounds really simple, but in practice, this is a hard model to get started. Paradigm shifts can take some time to get adopted. Again, lead by example. If others hold meetings that become more of a social event, or don't stay focused on an agenda and goal, roll with it. If you see others are getting frustrated, you could ask the meeting organizer if they achieved what they intended in the meeting. I'm not sure it would be a good idea to ask if the meeting was successful, but you might ask, "did you get the information you needed?". If they are receptive, you can suggest they might get better results by including an agenda and goal in their next meeting invite.

There is a difference between going to a meeting and being prepared for going to a meeting. If you are presenting a concept or an activity, especially to executives, you need to be prepared. I do this by taking some time to review the agenda of the meeting and consider what will be presented. If I'm presenting, I try to put myself (mentally) in the place of the executives I will be presenting to. Then I try to *anticipate* the questions they will ask when they receive the information I'm giving. I want to be prepared with the answers, should the question be asked. They might want to know projected costs, or interaction with other systems. Whatever it is, it will make you look good if you have answers ready.

Being a gardener (Plant the seeds...)

Continuing the thoughts on dealing with many different personalities I think we should look at another story...

In 1999, I was working for the Executive Office of the President (EOP) as the Network Manager for a major government support contract. I this role, I had a regular need to visit the White House and many of the other historical offices in the area. As technology improves throughout the years, certain infrastructure upgrades need to occur in order to support the newer technologies. By this time, we were moving from cable to fiber optics to the computer networking routers and switches. But there was a problem- these buildings are National Monuments. You can't just drill a whole to put in new wire runs. It literally takes an act of congress to get things approved. Okay, not literally, but it sure felt like it.

The value of making the change to fiber was like going from standard definition tv to High-Def. It would improve Internet speeds and data downloads. Everybody wanted it. The IT department worked with the Secret Service and a ton of other folks to figure out ways to get the fiber service installed without requiring any building modifications, and of course, still keeping the cables out of sight.

You probably know the White House is a busy place; full of political appointee's and interns. Every one of them believing that they are the second most important person in the building, having been appointed by the President himself. In most cases, that wasn't true. But that didn't stop them from acting like it.

My team and I worked late at night for many days, crawling through tight spaces, working in broom closets turned into telecommunications rooms and lifting carpets and reinserting them after the fiber cable was hidden. When the job was done, we waited to hear how the Executive staff enjoyed the improvements. Imagine our surprise when we overhear the Chief of Staff congratulating the IT Administrative Officer, a political appointee) for all the hard work and saying how he was going to recommend some sort of award. Not once did she acknowledge the team that did all the work. She didn't thank the cooperation of the Secret Service or the others that supported the effort. She didn't give credit to any of the dozens of people involved in the design, deployment or the testing. Nope. She said thank you to the Chief of Staff and then told him she was happy to help.

That had a demoralizing effect on the team. We busted our collective asses, only to have someone else take the credit!

People take credit for other's effort all of the time. It's sad, frustrating and demoralizing. Their motive is to make themselves look more effective, hardworking, or intelligent than others. The reality is that in most situations at work it's difficult to accurately assign who deserves credit. Even in situations where a leader does all the work, their staff had to take care of many other assignments to allow the leader the time to produce the new work.

Sure, there's a negative impact of taking credit for another person's work. The question is, are certain behaviors more affected by the taking − or giving − of credit? A study was conducted about the traits, good and bad, of leaders. It turns out, for leaders who took credit were in the bottom 10% versus those who were rated the highest in giving credit top 10%. Though many behaviors were listed, the negative impact of taking credit for others' work is clear. However, the focus should be on the extraordinary value that comes from giving others all the credit. Many people underestimate the impact that comes from making an effort to give credit to others.

Sometimes, in order to get an idea accepted, it has to come from the person in charge. Don't worry who that is. Everyone will know, because this is the kind of person who makes sure everyone knows he's in charge. I learned early on that I would have to deal with these kinds of people from time to time. They are authoritative leaders. They take all the credit. They want all of the attention. Look at me, I am in charge.

These people can be a pain to work for, but you have

a job to do and that means working with all types. So, how do you get the job done? You find out what it's going to take for them to look good in the eyes of their boss. Who do they report to? What is their mission? Once you know these things, you can start to find mutual areas of need. How can doing your job support his motivations? So, what happens when you need his support, but it won't directly benefit him? You need to get creative. You need to become a gardener.

Just as a gardener makes sure he has fertile soil, you will need to conscientiously create an environment where I'm in Charge feels comfortable. Make sure he is in his territory and is most likely to be receptive to hearing something you say. Now, you need to plant the seeds. You don't tell him your idea or need. You ask questions that lead him to seeing an area that needs attention. If he jumps on that train of thought, fine. If not, you can use passive language like, I wonder how they would react to that, or do you think that could help? You're just watering the seeds, waiting for them to sprout. I'm in Charge says, I have an idea. We should do THIS. He then proceeds to come somewhat close to what you wanted. You're going to act a little surprised and very interested. At this point, find a way to leave. Don't worry about the details or if he is exactly on target. You'll come back later and add some fertilizer.

While you are away, the tree you planted will start to grow. Contact him later and ask to discuss his idea in more detail. Go to him with YOUR plan, complete and the way YOU want it done. Give it to him and say that you liked his idea so much that you put this together for him. Tell him he can edit it to suit his needs, but please let you know how it turns out so I can be sure to keep you up to date on the effort. I'm in Charge will appreciate that you have everything planned out. I mean, if you already did the work, he doesn't have to. And besides, it's probably a better quality document than he would have made. He'll make small changes, so he can say he "fixed it", but the meat of the activity will stay the same. He likes it. It was his idea, after all.

Well, Fine.

Sometimes you just need to tell someone off. You are frustrated beyond words. You have had all you can take and you need a break. It's story time.

I served on the Battleship Wisconsin (BB-64) during the Desert Shield/Desert Storm era. It was the best unit ever. All of the crew wanted to be there. We were proud to be Battleship Sailors. I worked as a Fire Controlman in FA Division. We worked on the gun fire control systems that made sure the projectile hit the target. Using World War 2 technology, the Wisconsin could send a 16" round 18 miles with accuracy.

When you're in the Arabian Gulf (yeah, the Persian Gulf, they are the same place) and it's over 100 degrees every day, and you are waiting for the war to begin, even the best people can get irritable. On one such day our leading CPO, a Senior Chief named Sonny, was conducting zone inspections with the Department Head Officer. This guy was giving Sonny a hard time, picking over the simple things because he couldn't find anything really wrong. I mean really stupid things that had no bearing on our readiness. At the end of the inspection, the Department Head said, "Senior, I want all of these discrepancies resolved by 0800 and a complete report on my desk. Be ready for re-inspection." Senior Chief replied, "Well, Fine, Sir. Aye-Aye."

Another Chief, who was nearby let out a small snicker and quickly got the grin off of his face as the Department Head left our spaces. Senior Chief told us to turn to and get those discrepancies fixed right away. We wanted to get it done quick...Sonny was our Chief and we didn't want to let him down.

The next day we had the re-inspection and everything was fine. The Department Head didn't even conduct the inspection. He had our Division Officer do it. The Senior Chief was in a much better mood. Later I saw the Chief who had laughed at Sonny getting railed by the Department Head. I was kind of pissed about that and told him so. He busted out laughing at me. He said look, you're a smart guy. Did you ever take chemistry in school? Sure I did. So let me show you something. He took out his wheel book (notepad) and wrote:
Well Fine
That's what Senior Chief said to the Department Head, Right? Nothing offensive.
But look at it. In chemistry we break things down into more simple terms. Well Fine becomes-
WF
But that's not even simple enough. W is a compound, so that goes second, now you have-
FW
Still, there's more. W being a compound of two U's can be represented like this-
U2
So, what Senior said to the Department Head was-
FU2
Fuck You, too.
I had new respect for the Senior Chief.

You need to find a way to vent without getting yourself fired. You need to be careful of who you voice your frustrations to. Avoid complaining to coworkers or anyone who might know who you are complaining about. Share with your spouse, your dog, whatever. Be careful to be a positive force in the workplace. Say *Well Fine* if that works for you. Make up your own release. It doesn't matter. But the best way to win a confrontation is not to have it. Maintaining your composure goes a long way toward that goal.

Conflict Resolution

In business, just as in life, we don't always agree. At times, professionalism drops, and the knives come out. As a leader and a designated Un-F*er, it will be your job to keep people focused and working together toward your resolution. There are five generally accepted methodologies people use to resolve conflict:
- Avoiding: Some people hate confrontation so much they just choose to avoid it altogether. They choose this method because resultant stress of confrontation exceeds the reward of solving the conflict. For you, this might seem to make things easier, but people avoiding conflict aren't really contributing anything of value. In fact, they might be withholding worthwhile ideas. When conflict is avoided, nothing is resolved.
- Competing: Sometimes people just want to win. They're not cooperative, don't listen to others and can't conceive the idea they might be wrong. There's no room for diverse perspectives leading to a well-informed total picture. Good in a war, and football, but it's rarely a good strategy for group problem solving.
- Accommodating: Giving in, just to keep the peace. Being cooperative but not assertive. This may look gracious someone figures out s/he has been wrong about an argument. It's less helpful when one party accommodates another merely to preserve harmony or to avoid disruption. Like avoidance, it can result in

unresolved issues. Too much accommodation can result in groups where the most assertive parties commandeer the process and take control of most conversations.
- Collaborating: Used when people are both assertive and cooperative. The team lets each other contribute with the possibility of co-creating a shared solution that everyone can support.
- Compromising: Everyone gives up a little bit of what they want, and no one gets everything they want. The perception of the best outcome when working by compromise is that which "splits the difference." This might be viewed as being fair, but does anyone get what they want?

When we think about the different types of personalities we deal with, whether our bosses or our subordinate team members, you must expect that there will be conflict somewhere. From the business side, people will be interested in protecting their turf, their budget, their resources in general. This is all fine until it impacts your ability to complete a gate on your project of Un-F*cking the system.

To complicate things, you're also going to have to deal with Team Dynamics. If you are lucky and have good Team Leaders, they will take care of most of those issues. I wouldn't depend on it though. You need to create an environment that allows people to thrive in their job. Now is a good time to bring up the three things people need to stay in their current job.
1. Like what you do.
2. Like your co-workers
3. Get compensated appropriately

It sounds simple. To make it even easier, most people will continue on the job if they have only two out of the three. If you really like your job and you really like your compensation package, you might be willing to put up with some co-workers you don't care for. If you really like the people you work with and the job you have, maybe you will accept a little lower pay than you could get elsewhere. But If you don't think you're getting paid enough and you don't like your job, I don't care how much you like the people you work with. You are a flight risk.

Think about these things when you talk to your team, as part of getting to know them. Ask the three questions and learn where each person stands. If needed, you can look to resolving some of those issues. If you want to keep them, that is.

Back to conflict- What do you do when you have a disrupter? There are many different types of disruptive behavior. These are things that make a work environment difficult. As with many other areas in this book, there are plenty of places to read and learn about how to deal with these people. I'm not talking about the obnoxious dude, the loud talker or the person who really needs a bar of soap. I'm talking about people who disrupt *your* project. If you need to learn how to deal with the other issues, there are tons of books and articles on the subject.

We're going to deal with the disruptions to your efforts.

If you are not part of the solution, you're part of the problem.

You're likely to discover conflict or a disruptor when you are informed of a roadblock to an activity. The logical question in your mind will be "What is the roadblock and what does it effect?". The "why" evaluation comes next. In many cases, the why will be a "who" and not a "what". This means someone or a group of someone's are impacting your project. It's time for you to put on your Super Un- F'cker cape and fix this.

Identify the individual or group that is being a blocker.

Your Gatekeeper should be able to tell you, but if not, you're going to ask around until you know who it is. You want to create an opportunity to have an informal discussion with them. Ideally, the discussion is done with some privacy. You want to approach this by asking questions about their effort. Gain an understanding about the importance of their job/task or whatever. Be empathetic, share your understanding and show that you value what they are doing. Even if you don't, make them feel that you do.

When they feel that you respect, value and appreciate their work, they will be psychologically obligated to treat your efforts with the same respect. Explain your end goal (what project you are getting back on track, etc.) and who your sponsor and stakeholders are. Share how their activities are creating a roadblock to your success. Ask the easy question: "Can you help?". If the answer is no, the next question is "Who has the authority to make a decision that would help resolve this roadblock?". The goal here is not really to resolve anything as much as identify who has the authority to aid in a resolution. Maybe it's the next person in the upward chain of command. Mabey it will turn out that your sponsor also has overall accountability for their project as well.

Eventually you will find someone with decision making ability. You will pose the risks to you project and the reasons why you need the roadblock cleared. You will explain the impact to the other project and the ideas why they don't want to support your effort. Notice the different language here. You have *reasons*, they have *ideas*. Remember, you are using persuasive communications to get what you need to get your job done. You may need to compromise. Have some alternative thoughts in mind before you go into this discussion. This is negotiation. You are going to start with what you want and hope you get it just by stating the facts. If that fails, provide some more palatable ideas. You may have to change your completion gate a few days instead of a few weeks. Maybe some overtime could be used. Semper Gumby- be prepared to be flexible. Plan for Failure, know what you will do if you are unsuccessful in your negotiations.

There are going to be times when people simply whine. You need to be able to measure the difference between a whiney personality and someone who is passively trying to voice a complaint. Generally, a little whininess is okay. When it spreads, and everyone is doing it there's a problem. A social hour can be helpful to you to find out what are on the minds of people. Go back to asking the three questions to gauge how they like their job/co-workers/pay. You may find a common thread that needs attention. Another method is to get a few of the leaders in a room and have a bitch session. Those events need to be just a very few people and focused on issues of morale and overall team welfare. Maybe there is a ring-leader to the whining. Then what will you do?

It happens. You either adopted an incumbent employee, or you hired someone you shouldn't have. Whatever the case, this person is creating a disruption to the team. You must fix it, because it can become a cancer. It can cause people not to like their co-workers, which causes people to look for a new job. If people quit, your program is in jeopardy of failing.

Your communications skills are going to come into play again. There are many ways to deal with these situations. Picking the way that best suits your purpose and the personality traits of the disruptor will have a direct impact on your successful resolution of the issue. You may need to discuss this with your sponsor. Explain the impact to the project if things are not changed, then your plan to fix it. Get buy in, approval. If not that, then at least acknowledgement that you are handling things.

You may need to involve HR. Go with your company policy on that.

Before you confront the person, you need to identify the specific behaviors and/or actions that are causing a problem. State exactly how this has a negative impact on the project. Ask if your assessment makes sense to them or if there is something you missed. Notice I didn't say "or if you were wrong about something" – you aren't trying to have a right vs wrong discussion. You are discussing observations. Come to an agreement on the fact that when things adversely effect the project, I'm the one held accountable. It's my job to identify risks and resolve them. Once that understanding is created and the risks to the program identified, you have to ask the next logical question.

"We both agree there are issues impacting the program. We both agree that it is my responsibility to resolve or mitigate risks to the program. You are a valuable member of the team and your contributions are appreciated. But we need to focus on ways to fix this situation. Let's start our first approach by working together. What are your ideas for fixing this?"

You then go point by point through the issues identified. You want the individual to make recommendations and to take some ownership on changing behavior. If there are areas where you have to put forth corrective measures, try to get buy in by asking, "does this make sense as a resolution?" until you get concurrence.

After the discussion, you thank them for their help in coming up with a plan. You let them know that you will be following up your meeting with an e-mail detailing your agreement. You let them know that you will be watching the specific areas of activity to monitor the success.

If all goes well and the behaviors that caused the issue are resolved, you rock. If all your efforts were wasted and the behaviors don't improve, or maybe even worsen, you need to take stronger action. For your next meeting, you need a witness. You need to coordinate with HR. You need to have documented your first meeting and now have examples of what actions you both agreed on and what did and did not get accomplished. You are now going from engendering a cooperative engagement to a directive engagement. This meeting is going to be a performance improvement plan implementation.

You will specifically re-iterate each risk to the program you both identified and the activity you agreed on to mitigate them. You will identify where work has occurred and show sincere appreciation for those efforts. Where there are shortfalls, you will state your findings on the remaining risk. You will provide them with an opportunity to explain why the agreed action was not taken. No matter what the excuse is, the information was not communicated to you prior to the meeting, so you must put it into the improvement plan.

Each activity now must have a suspense date (done no later than). There must be a monitoring method to track the activity. There must be a way to measure or define the "done" state.

Bottom line- The success of this program depends on you to do your job, and specifically, these tasks. Your failure to complete these requirements in the time specified could result in disciplinary actions, possibly termination. (depending on your company policies, of course)

It has been my experience that one of two things will happen next. Either they take it seriously and get the job done, or they float their resume and try to get a new job before they get fired. If they quit or get fired, you need to move on. Tell your existing staff that you gave opportunity for resolution, but in the end, it didn't work out. Share what you and the former employee agreed to and ask if there are any places someone might take up the slack. Ask if anyone knows someone who would be a good backfill. Always better to get someone on the team that is already known and liked by at least one other person.

CHAPTER 8

I WANT TO BE THE EMPORER
(EMPIRICAL DATA RULES!)

Throughout this book I have talked about concepts that often deal with change. If there is a problem, you first look at what changed. If you are trying to get a different outcome, you need to implement change. If you need to correct behavior, you need to define change. If you want to try out improvements, you need to evaluate the change. The title of this chapter refers to empirical data. I love data. It's just the facts, and it doesn't lie.

I use a system I call 3M to build my requirements to manage change. They are:
- Measure
- Monitor
- Manage

Empirical data is information that is used to make decisions. When you think about the 3M's, you might get a little overwhelmed at first. I don't want anyone overwhelmed. Or underwhelmed, for that matter. I want everyone in a comfortable state of whelmed. Story time, again...

The National Oceanic and Atmospheric Administration (NOAA) is an American scientific agency within the United States Department of Commerce that focuses on the conditions of the oceans, major waterways, and the atmosphere. They have a really big computer networking system. There are many components within the organization and most are tasked with managing their portions of the interconnected system. As a contracting

Director of Programs overseeing many activities within NOAA I was responsible for assuring the programs and projects were providing the required support to the NOAA components. One of these was the National Oceans Service (NOS).

NOS was having a problem. They experienced network slow-downs, outages and other issues and folks were getting tired of it. The IT staff always jumped through the hoops to get things fixed, and they could usually say what caused the problem. But they didn't seem able to stop the issues from happening in the first place. The Chief Information Officer (CIO) was being held accountable to his boss, and we all know how shit runs down-hill.

The CIO and other leaders knew that they had spent a ton of money on commercially developed systems monitoring tools. They had security tools, network management tools and log scanning tools. They knew these tools were among the best available and were completely capable of doing the job. Yet, the failures continued to occur. They wanted answers. What they wanted even more was a solution.

On the surface you would say their tools weren't working. The purpose of the tools was to monitor the systems for anomalies that would indicate an impending problem and create an alert so that technicians could take corrective actions before a failure occurred. When we started digging into what was going on, we found that the alerts were happening as they were designed to. So, what was the problem?

It wasn't that the system monitoring tools didn't work. In fact, they worked really well. Maybe too well? When we got down to the level of the IT technicians that were doing the job, they already knew what the problem was. When they showed me a report from just one of the monitoring tools, I could see the issue, too. In one day, there were over 700,000 alerts. The techs couldn't see the forest for the trees. Somewhere in the reports was the information that would have alerted the impending system failures.

The concept of one-size-fits all is usually BS. Just like a suit bought off the rack might require a trip to the tailor to get the best fit, monitoring tools need to be adapted to your environment. I've been talking about IT situations, but the concepts apply to anything that you want/need to measure, monitor and manage. You don't need to monitor everything just because you can. What should you monitor then?

You need to think about what you need to know. What information would be actionable? Why are you monitoring it? In other words, why would you monitor something if you couldn't set an alert that would trigger an activity?

We talked about a six-step troubleshooting method at the beginning of this book. At one point, we discussed problem indicators. Power on/off lights, service engine lamps and things like that. Wouldn't it be helpful if we had those indicators in business? That's what 3M is all about. In engineering circles, we talk about Specifications and Metrics. Specifications are quantitative, measurable criteria that the product is designed to satisfy. To be measurable and unambiguous, specifications must contain a metric, target value and engineering units for the target value. The metric is the characteristic of the product that will be measured.

I get it. Geek speak. Let me see if I can clear this up some. Contemplate that you want to make a change to a system, perhaps to fix a problem or make a performance improvement. You need to be able to evaluate if the change provided the result you expected. If you don't have this data, how can you know, or empirically prove, that the change worked? When a proposal is made to rectify a problem, or a suspected problem, it really does need to be a *proposal*.

What should a change proposal look like? Just a clarification first. This is not a "Change Request". That comes after a proposal is agreed upon. For now, we're going to create, or as a leader, direct to be created, a document that sells the change proposed. The proposal will start off by stating the current (or as-is) state, pointing out a deficiency. The next section will detail your proposed activity (the change) that you will implement to rectify the deficiency. The following section of the proposal will describe how you intend to validate that the change activity was effective in resolving the deficiency. The last section will describe what activity will be required in the event the change was not successful, perhaps uninstalling the change or reverting to the prior state.

At this point in our discussion, I'm hoping that you will see the value in defining specific metrics that will provide actionable information. You want to be able to prove the changes had the desired effect, or you want to have evidence that a system is performing as it was designed to. This all goes back to requirements gathering and knowing the definition of "done". How will you know when you are successful? Have empirical data to prove it.

Now let's talk about some operational aspects of 3M. When you have completed your job of finding the problem and implementing an effective, proven change (fix), you don't just leave. You need to establish a 3M plan that will provide for the ongoing assurance of continued system performance. You also want to provide for a method to implement and enable continuous process improvement (CPI).

This might be a good time for thinking about how you got here. Here- the place where something was so broken that you needed to be called in to fix it. Here is where you are because things change. People change, adds to systems happen. Systems and processes are developed to support a need without real thought to follow-on activities. Organizational change leaves systems and processes orphaned with no oversite. Programs are put in place without any thought of a baseline or a process to monitor changes and impacts. You are here because you know how to make things right. Because you have the ability to learn how a system should perform (was intended, did at one time) or more importantly, how your sponsor expects and wants it to perform. You will take that information and create a statement that describes the expectations of the system performance and get agreement from the sponsor(s) and stakeholders. Then you will define criteria (metrics) that will prove that the required performance indicators are being met.

In the end, you see, is a system that provides a warm, fuzzy blanket of confidence that the system you fixed continues to operate and meet the expectations defined in the performance requirements. Not only that, but you have put into place a monitoring program that will continue to report on the metrics that show the health of the system, a method to make and monitor the effectiveness of corrective maintenance and process improvement changes and alert the appropriate people when certain thresholds occur so that corrective actions can be made.

If all of that activity had been done, and continued, in the first place, you wouldn't be here now.

I do want to talk some more about 3M and some considerations you will want to make when setting up or tweaking a monitoring system or tool.

The image above shows a sample of a systems

monitoring dashboard element. In real life, there would be an arrow (speedometer type) showing where in the green, yellow or red area the performance indicators were, in this case, averaged over a month. Note the simplicity here. Green is good, red is bad. Labels are clearly indicated. You can put in whatever terminology that will make sense to the customer of the dashboard. Create these things from the viewpoint of the intended audience.

We know that we only want to monitor the things that will provide us with actionable metrics, but does everyone need to see all that is being monitored? The people who maintain a system will probably want a different set of reports than the people who use the system. Leaders and executives may want their own dashboard report to stay on top of things. I prefer to provide static reports to customers and executive while reserving dynamic, real-time reports for systems SME's. I do this because anomalies in performance can be viewed as emergencies if the data is not understood.

How should we decide what to measure and report on? As stated earlier, we need to monitor those areas or functions of a system that indicate performance is within design specification. Proof that everything is as it should be. It won't always be easy to determine what needs to be measured to provide proof, but it is important to do. If your system is a complex one, break it into logical functional areas and find places to put "test points". These can be very helpful in troubleshooting down the road (Everything works fine up to this point in the system. Logically, there's something going on before we get here). From the system owner/maintainer perspective, you want to identify and monitor indicators that will show you the health of the system.

Think about a household Wi-Fi network. The system you bought is rated at 80Mbps upload and 50Mbps download. That's pretty good. But things seem slow, so you run a speed test and find out you're only getting 70/38 instead of 80/50 that you are paying for. Are you going to call your service provider and complain, or at this point, do you just accept it and hope it gets better? Or maybe you refresh your connections, search for other devices in your home that might be sucking up bandwidth, whatever. Would your reaction be different if your speed test indicated 12/10 instead? Is that your tolerance level, or somewhere in between? At what point does action need to be taken?

Every system needs to have a user tolerance level defined for each of the expected performance areas. This can be arbitrary, based on experience in dealing with complaints. A better way might be through user acceptance testing. The point is, you need to know the point at which performance degradations turn into negative customer impact. Semper Gumby here- you may need to adjust based on changing tolerance levels over time.

The target for this activity isn't so much to define when customers get upset as it is to define a metric for an alert notification. You don't want to sit around all day monitoring systems, especially when everything is working right. But you do want to be notified when things are degrading to a level that may impact the customer experience. You need to set alert thresholds. When a monitoring system measuring metric reaches a certain parameter, it triggers action.

The key word here is action. The entire purpose of the 3M system is to provide *actionable* information. This is one of those areas where you think back to planning for failure. When a threshold is reached, and an alert triggered, who will get the alert? What activity should they do? Who should they communicate with? How long do they have to react? What you are trying to do here is to have a pre-defined activity that will restore the system to a point below the alert threshold. If you get too many of the same alert, it may be an indicator that the current system resources need upgraded. Lucky for you, you have empirical data to use as justification for the upgrade. If alerts are happening too frequently and don't require action, you should consider changing the threshold. Just be sure the timeliness of the alert allows for the required actions to occur before the alert becomes an alarm.

If an alert means, "hey, pay attention" then an alarm means "**HEY, PAY ATTENTION!!**" The audience will be different on an alarm. This is going to the people who need to know when something breaks. This is something that has direct impact or requires immediate action. An alarm triggers a communications plan that was agreed upon when the monitoring system was configured. When deciding who to include on alarm notifications, you need to consider what activity each person will be required to take. It is possible that some will be Keep Informed Only while others will have specific actions to take.

Post alarm activity will include an after action report and a root cause analysis. The goal will be to document what action was taken after the alarm. Was the action plan followed? Was it effective? What caused the alarm? Was there an alert first? What was the root cause and contributors that resulted in the alarm? What changes can be implemented so this is less likely to happen in the future?

CHAPTER 9

IT'S NOT YOU, IT'S ME

Sometimes things just don't go the way you plan. It's possible for you to do everything right and still not be able to fix it. The problem might be too deeply ingrained in the psyche of the organization. Maybe someone, or a group of someone's, is undermining your efforts. Maybe people are lying to you about things. It could be you just sucked this time. It does happen.

Whatever the reason, when you find that you have failed to complete your objectives, your behavior will be critical to your future. I already know that this will be the most difficult chapter to write. Telling people how to do the right things is a lot easier than the introspection required to talk about when things go wrong.

If things are going wrong, it won't come as a surprise. You will know. You are missing gates, the meetings with sponsors and stakeholders are becoming tedious and unenjoyable. Your reports cause you stress because you know that the news in them isn't what people want to hear. You probably stopped having fun a while ago. Your team knows things aren't going well, too. They can tell in your demeanor. What are you going to do?

Every situation is different, but there will be some things that just didn't get the attention that was needed. You may have read someone's motivations wrong or perhaps they changed without you realizing it. You may not have understood or been able to adapt to the political intrigue that is so prevalent in today's work place. In some cases, it's better to walk away so that you can fight another day. In the event you get terminated, you're going to need to do some real soul searching to figure out why. And yes, it was your fault. Deal with it.

There is a saying that I'm fond of. "All things in moderation, including moderation." Semper Gumby is a real motto for me. I discovered early on that I am nowhere near as good as I thought I was. Sure, I had some great success stories to tell. But when it came right down to it I couldn't do nearly as much as the people I was working with. I was beginning to feel like I was a fraud. Then my best friend told me, "You're in paradise. Stop bitching and enjoy the day." It really never was all about me. It was about the people I surrounded myself with. The incredibly talented engineers, customer service people, the administrators and clerks and team leads. They were who made me look good.

I learned that you can't do everything. But as a leader whose primary function is to unscrew things up, you need to get people to want to work for you. Sure, you need to know enough that you won't get bamboozled, but you don't need to be the expert on everything.

Once you recognize that you don't have to be the expert in all things, it allows you to depend on others. People will see that you value what they do and what they have to contribute. Now, early in my teambuilding efforts, I make it a point to *tell* people that I don't know everything. In fact, I might know just enough to put my foot in my mouth. If we're in a meeting together and I say something that isn't true, please rescue me. I'd prefer you do it politely, but I will appreciate it. I have my fair share of stories where I wish I had been rescued!

The things that de-rail your best laid plans tend to be more social issues than technical ones. The planning and understanding of how things work or how we expect things to work isn't the hard part. If you look at users manuals or think about training courses, they almost always are focused on how things work. The best manuals might have a couple trouble shooting thoughts at the end. But, more often than not, no thought is given on what to do when the system isn't working the way it's expected.

There will be situations where your technical approach is flawed. Hopefully, those will be discovered early on and you can adjust as needed. In the Agile software development approach they follow a concept called "Fail fast, fail often". The key word there isn't fail, it's fast. The unspoken idea is to *learn fast*. Experiment and figure out what does and doesn't work. Quickly adjust and move on. I'm not sure I'd use this tactic in building bombs (failing early could be the end of the project), but there are a lot of places where this does make sense. But let's examine some of the social issues that can lead to failure.

Nobody likes me

Could that really be the case? I mean, you're a nice enough person, right? But if you view yourself from the perspective of others, you may come to realize that people might have a reason not to like you. The reason is pretty basic. The very fact that you are there to fix things means that things *need* to be fixed. If you are successful when things had failed, the implication is that they failed. It creates a vested interest that you *not be successful*.

On the other hand, I have found this concept to be helpful. There are different situations where you can be hired. In one situation, someone has done really well and has been promoted or is moving on to some other effort and they are looking for a backfill. Another situation might be that things have gone well, a few problems here and there, but mostly good results. The incumbent is leaving for a new role. The third situation is not so pretty. There are a lot of problems, missed timelines and budget overruns. The incumbent is being moved out because they want to "move in a new direction".

Which of these situations would you want to step into? Which do you think is the safest for your career? If you take the position where the incumbent was a superstar, you have some big shoes to fill. You will be constantly compared to them. They will have created deep relationships with the stakeholders and those will be lasting. The best you can hope for is to be as good as the last guy. Anything less, and you will be viewed as "just okay" or worse. Maybe you like a role where things are pretty good, and you just need to maintain status quo. The second example might be satisfying to you. There are some areas where you can bring improvements. But for me, I always look for the third example. In the best-case scenario, you are the savior and the superstar. You have challenges and have proven your worth by fixing what was wrong. In the worst-case situation, you were no worse than the person you replaced.

That's all well and good, but you do need to deal with the real possibility that people might be opposed to you coming in to save the day. You are going to need to overcome that challenge to be successful. No, you do not need everyone to like you to be a success, but it sure does make things easier. How you will win people over to support you will be challenging, and different methods will need to be employed for different personalities and situations. Is it possible that some situations are insurmountable? Of course. You can't win every time. But hopefully, you will be able to get enough people to cooperate to make the changes that are needed to fix the issues.

You need to first examine if there is something about your behavior that is creating animosity. I know that, if you are reading this book, you have a strong personality. To do this kind of work, you must. You are going to be driven to get things done, and that means making changes. But are you plowing others over in your attempts to get things done? Remember that people will be invested in their ways. The have expended effort and don't want it to be all for nothing. If you feel that your ideas and concepts are not being accepted, then you need to re-evaluate your communications. How are you being perceived? Are you viewed as someone who is trying to help or as a troublemaking burden?

Be aware of habits that can turn people off. Are you a good listener? Even if you don't agree with someone, if you want them to listen to you then you need to listen to their views. Keep in mind that opinions are just that; personal thoughts generally based on emotions and experience. If someone told you their favorite color was green, you're not going to argue that its really blue. The same should hold true with concepts and approaches to problems.

Earlier in the book I talked about brainstorming sessions for defining a critical path. If you are having trouble getting buy-in for your ideas because a few people just don't seem to like you then it would be a good idea to hold a group discussion on the ideas. The first thing to do is declare the end state you are trying to achieve. This must be in the form of a positive sentence that tells a benefit. For example:

"The new air-conditioning system must be less than 2 decibels loud within five feet of the unit. This will result in higher customer satisfaction, being more competitive in the retail market, and increased sales"

Get everyone to agree that the goal is valid, even if they don't think it is realistic or achievable. Notice that it is a positive statement. It didn't indicate the flawed design or the bad choice of fan or anything like that. Just the goal to make it better.

The next step will be to get people to make suggestions on how to improve. Even if you already know the path you want to follow, let them come up with ideas. For one thing, they might come up with something good that you didn't consider. For another thing, if they think it's their idea, they will be more receptive than if you tell them. If you know that there are a few ring leaders that don't want to see you succeed, divide the group into teams and make sure you have a champion for you on each team that can counteract the negativity.

Here are some bad habits to be careful of:
- Interrupting
- Finishing peoples sentences for them
- Demeaning or belittling ideas
- Publicly criticizing anyone
- Being dismissive

Good Habits to focus on:
- Be an ACTIVE listener
- Plant seeds of ideas so others can claim them as ideas of their own
- Accept ideas and opinions as what they are.
- Offer questions instead of opposition
- Praise Publicly, but always sincerely

You're not going to be everyone's friend. But with a little effort, you should be able to get cooperation for completing tasks that you can show value to, even if the only value is that once done you will leave them alone.

Incumbent attitudes

What's an incumbent? It's the staffing that you adopt when you come aboard. Any staff you bring with you or acquire later are not incumbents. So, why would their attitudes be a concern? How can they program me for failure?

It turns out that the incumbent staff can a great asset. These people have been in the organization longer than you have. Some maybe a great deal longer. They know the secrets, the personalities, the history and the environment all better than you will. Unfortunately, this knowledge can be used against you. One of my biggest pet-peeves ever is a knowledge hog. People who have defined their value by the knowledge they hold and create their job security through wielding it. These people are typically arrogant in their approach to business relationships. They look down on others and create animosity everywhere they go. Sadly, you will need these people on your side. Eventually they can be turned around to become mentors, but that is a time demanding effort. For getting projects done, you need them. Try not to piss them off too soon.

Another way incumbents can cause trouble is by willfully keeping you ignorant. They don't share things with you that you should know about the business environment or a specific system because they want you to fail. In their minds, if you fix things that they didn't, you threaten their position. Be sure to include the incumbent staff in planning sessions. It's a good idea to conduct one-on-one meetings early on to learn their personalities, their areas of expertise, what they think could be better (What would you change if…), and what their future goals are.

A good practice is to ask, "What do you think you are best at, enjoy doing the most?" and also, "What tasks do you wish you didn't have to do? What do you feel like you don't have the best skills doing?" If you know these details, you can work to accentuate the positive and minimize the negatives. In business terms, you want to apply the resources you have to the best of their capabilities, leaving the tasks they are not great at to others.

We always do it this way

An incumbent trait, although not limited in any way to incumbents alone, is the idea that you can't do something different. You are an agent for change. People resist change. It's in our very nature. If we have done something that has worked for years and was good enough, why change? It's a good thing cell phone companies don't follow this philosophy. We'd all still use a flip phone. But that doesn't make it less of a challenge.

Resistance to change can come in the form foot-dragging, sabotage or even rebellion. There are a lot of reasons for the resistance Each reason should be identified, examined, and viewed as a risk to your efforts. Mitigation plans then are developed, discussed and implemented.
Causes of Change Resistance:
- *Loss of Control-* When others (you) drive change, people can feel like they have lost the control of their responsibilities. Keeping them well informed and included can help this issue.
- *Excess Uncertainty-*Better the devil you know...Many people would rather to continue in an uncomfortable situation than risk uncertainty. You need to provide a sense of safety and inspiring vision. Process, workflows, timelines are all things we use to reduce uncertainty.
- *Surprise-* Snap decisions foisted ono people are welcomed enthusiastically. Seek input before springing an unexpected change.
- *Everything is different-* Remember the concept of the ant and the elephant? The same goes for change. Small bites at a time are easier to digest. Too much change at once can be both overwhelming and confusing.
- *Loss of ownership-* Even if it's the ownership of something that didn't work, people are likely to be invested in it. You can try to help people maintain dignity by celebrating a system's past with a decommissioning ceremony, pointing out the good

things done and the great things to come.
- *Loss of ability-* "I knew that system inside and out. Now it's changing and I'm not sure I'm ready for it." Plan for training and overlap (run old and new in parallel) can mitigate these concerns.
- *It Hurts!-*In some cases, the reality is change will hurt. Some jobs may become obsolete. Some revenue streams may break. You need to be honest about the expectations up front. People are going to figure it out, so own it up front. Why was the decision made? What are you (the company) going to do to ease the pain? Training, new positions, help finding a new role, etc.

Stakeholder apathy

Stakeholders are people, or an organization, that can be positively or negatively impacted by a project outcome. They could also be a stakeholder if they have the capacity to have an impact on that project. We can typically group these three ways:
- Primary stakeholders – those affected by the outcome of the project.
- Secondary stakeholders – those that are indirectly affected by the outcome or progress of the project
- Key stakeholders – those that fall into neither of the other categories but still have significant ability to influence the project or the business

These are the people or organizations that need to be happy with your performance. Usually, these are the folks your sponsor is responsible to. You will face differently motivated stakeholders. Some will be driven with high interest in your project and have high power to support you. Others, less so. These are champions for your success. They are vested in seeing you complete the project. You need to nurture and maintain that relationship.

Unfortunately, you will also have to deal with apathetic stakeholders. These people may have a passive interest in what you are doing. As long as everything is going well they will be quietly supportive. Beware, however, the moment something goes south. These folks will be the first to call for you head. Although they may not have much actual power, it's the squeaky wheel that gets the grease. You will do well to be aware of who your apathetic stakeholders are and create friendships where you can.

Sponsor fails to support

This doesn't happen very often. In most cases, certainly in the beginning, your sponsor will be your biggest supporter. They want to see you succeed because they are quite literally invested in your success. Occasionally, though, things can take a change for the worse. Business needs may have changed. Leadership may have changed. Funding might get pulled. There are many reasons you might lose sponsor support. Frankly, when they happen, you're pretty much done. Put on your salesman hat and do your best to justify your projects existence. Time to float that resume.

Expectations exceed possible reality

Sometimes a project is doomed to fail because the desired outcome is more of an idea than an achievable reality. I've seen this happen a few times in the research and development arena. There are actually places where the business model is to fail at least a certain percentage in order to be sure the envelope is being pushed far enough. In other situations, designers want to do things that they simple "believe" can be achieved with technology or some other resource. Never mind that they don't have an understanding of the resource they anticipate using. In you role you will need to evaluate the requirements of a project and be sure that it fits into the art of the possible. We get challenges; those are fun. But you don't want to spend tons of time, money and brain cycles trying to complete a project that will never deliver the desired outcomes.

In situations like this you should not just throw in the towel. Instead, you need to re-baseline the project goals and requirements. State clearly what can and cannot be accomplished. Where possible, identify workarounds. If a goal is unachievable due to constraints other than technical capability, such as time line or budget, make a case for what can be achieved within the constraints. Be ready to address what you would need in order to deliver the project with full requirements. If it would take more time, be ready to explain why and how much. Same goes for budget or scope.

Inability to get key support at the moment it is needed most

This kind of situation can be devastating to you and your program. In these situations, everything will have been going well. The things that you planned have been coming to fruition just as you expected. For the next gate in the critical path, you need the resources of someone outside of your control. Let's use a security group for example here. You are the person who is going to get a delinquent program back on schedule. We'll say it's at an airport, and your next Critical Path Gate is to get TSA approval for your security plan. Until the plan is approved, your team cannot begin construction.

Your team has followed every requirement and the package is complete and sitting with TSA. You have scheduled labor to begin on the construction starting on Monday, but here it is Friday, two weeks after you submitted the required documentation, and you still haven't heard from TSA on their approval. You're going to have to re-schedule the construction labor, probably lose money on that. You're going to have to find ways to adjust your timelines to make up for the delay. More money lost. You're going to have to go back to the stakeholders and sponsors to tell them about the delay. I sure wouldn't want to be you.

How can you overcome this kind of roadblock? You probably won't be able to, so I hope you built a little cushion into your timeline. I would recommend that when you are building your critical path and assigning responsibility for each Gate (Gatekeepers), you need to examine what level of control you have over the activity. You need to identify those places where you are dependent upon the activities of others. It may be that these other groups are stakeholders outside your purview but have a vested interest in your projects success. Those resources need to be communicated with often concerning the value that they will provide to the project and continuous confirmation of the completion of their assigned tasks.

The really dangerous situation to your project is when the resources outside of your control do not have a vested interest in the projects success. They don't care if you succeed or fail. So you are truly dependent on them to do their job. How can you ensure that they will get the job done when you need it to be done? If you have identified the dependency soon enough, you may be able to negotiate a service agreement (contract) in advance of the award of the services required. In lieu of that, continuous communications and monitoring of the job activities is all you can hope for. These dependencies, where you have little or no control, need to be identified, documented, and shared with the sponsors and where appropriate, the stakeholders. A mitigation plan should be discussed as a plan for failure activity. You may not be able to stop it from happening, but you can have a plan in place that reduces the impact. You can have the risk analysis and mitigation plan reviewed and approved by your sponsor and stakeholders so that they are not surprised if the situation pops up.

Irrefutable Logic

Okay, story time-

"Well, ya see, Norm, it's like this. A herd of buffalo can only move as fast as the slowest buffalo. And when the herd is hunted, it is the slowest and weakest ones at the back that are killed first. This natural selection is good for the herd as a whole, because the general speed and health of the whole group keeps improving by the regular killing of the weakest members! In much the same way, the human brain can only operate as fast as the slowest brain cells. Excessive intake of alcohol, as we know, kills brain cells. But naturally, it attacks the slowest and weakest brain cells first. In this way, regular consumption of beer eliminates the weaker brain cells, making the brain a faster and more efficient machine! That's why you always feel smarter after a few beers."
From Cheers, season 2, episode 1

Just because something sounds logical doesn't mean it's true. You will be fielding ideas and arguments that come from the individuals point of view. You have to listen to these ideas, approaches and viewpoints because, as we have discussed, you don't know everything. But just because someone said something that made sense doesn't mean that it's fit for the project that you are doing. When people come to you with ideas that they want to implement in the project, you need to consider the following:
- Will it support the requirements of the project (outcome)?
- Will it change tasking?
- Will it be disruptive to current activities?
- Will it be seen as a value add to the rest of the resources (people doing the work)?

Read this:

> 1N73LL1G3NC3 15
> 7H3 4B1L17Y
> 70 4D4P7 70 CH4NG3

Do you see it? It's a quote from Steven Hawking. Intelligence is the ability to adapt to change. Our minds are very flexible in this way. I include this example in this book because it helps to point out that our brains will often fill in the blanks to make us believe what we expect to see as opposed to what is actually there.

When we have certain expectations, it is natural to look for evidence that meet our anticipations. This is a case where "Trust but Verify" comes to being important. But more so, we need to gauge our expectations of the people we work with. You will always be disappointed when you expect people to act as you would. As a leader, though, you shouldn't expect anything from anyone that you wouldn't be willing to do yourself. Don't expect everyone to agree with you. In fact, encourage different viewpoints.

Be careful that you don't miss things that are glaring to others. When you write an important email, get someone else to read it before you send. At minimum, read it out loud yourself. Do peer reviews on project activities instead of just signing them off as done. Including more sets of eyes in the review will reduce errors by orders of magnitude.

Confirmation bias is when we look for, evaluate, favor, and remember information in a way that supports our beliefs. It is a type of cognitive bias and an error of reasoning. People show this bias when they gather or remember information selectively, seeing only things that support their point. For example, people who believe in UFO's might only look at the evidence that supports their beliefs and ignore evidence that suggests what they think is a UFO was a weather balloon.

You need to be careful of confirmation bias in yourself and others. It can derail your project by making you start to assume things are what you want them to be rather than what they are. When building your project objectives and defining what outcomes are expected, make sure that you use a 3M approach to measure-with empirical data-the proof that your project provides the expected, required outcomes.

Sweat-Ex, or Stressing out

"We're making the same mistakes we made 1,000 years ago. So they must be the right ones. So relax."
-Chuck Palahniuk

Sweat Ex, or sweat exercise, is a military term for applying maximum stress to a training event. It's done to prepare troops for the emotional and physical realities of conflicts. In business, it's highly unlikely that we will ever experience those kinds of situations, but the level of stress we put on ourselves is often comparable to the amount of stress provided in those military exercises. In this section, we examine both your stress and the stress of the people you will work with. I'm sure you know it is important to manage your stress levels, but did you know that you can influence the stress management of others?

First, stress is not always a negative thing. There are positive effects caused by stress that can be useful to you. Stress causes a burst of energy that advises you on what to do. Limited stress has many benefits. Stress can help you achieve your everyday commitments and motivates you to reach your goals. In fact, stress can help you accomplish tasks more efficiently. It can even boost memory.

Stress also produces the fight-or-flight instinct response. When the brain perceives stress, it releases chemicals like epinephrine, norepinephrine and cortisol.

This creates a variety of reactions including an increase in blood pressure and heart rate. The senses suddenly have a laser-like focus, so you can avoid physically stressful situations - such as dodging a thrown snowball or jumping away from a car - and be safe.

Unfortunately, sustained, long-term stress can have a deleterious effect on our minds and bodies. It can weaken our immune systems, tire us out and create anxiety. Some of the signs that you are experiencing too much stress are:

- Inability to concentrate or complete tasks
- Get sick more often with colds
- Body aches
- Other illnesses like autoimmune diseases flare up
- Headaches
- Irritability
- Trouble falling sleeping or staying awake
- Changes in appetite
- More angry or anxious than usual

Some people, myself included, seem to do their best work under a certain level of stress. Others quickly degrade, getting flustered and nervous. You will have to watch for these signs so that you get the best performance out of yourself and your team. Examine what causes the stress in your business environment. How about in your specific project or program? I know that there are a few things that consistently come up. The overwhelming first place is time.

Deadlines- it just sounds ominous, doesn't it? Throughout this book I have talked about managing activity based on the achievement of a task. Not on setting a timeline. This can be confusing to people who have always had to manage to timelines. I understand this but hear me out. If you must, give your sponsor the dates needed to manage budget and reports. You will want to put a reasonable amount of padding into these timelines to be able to adapt to unforeseen delays. If you have a great relationship with your sponsor, you might want to provide them with a Best, Most Likely, and Worse Case list of possible end dates. These dates should not be shared with the team in general.

In 1955, Cyril Northcote Parkinson wrote an essay in *The Economist* talking about his experience in the British civil service. His first sentence became known as "Parkinson's Law".

"Work expands so as to fill the time available for its completion"

What this means is that if you give someone a week to submit a report that could be done in two days, they will use the week to complete it. Not the two days. In reality, they will probably wait until the last possible moment to do the work instead of spreading it out over the week. If you provide the timeline for the completion dates of critical path gates and other objectives, the focus becomes those dates instead of the objectives. When I first began my career in project management, people would report their status as percentages of completion. Most PM software tools, like Gant Charts, are based on the combination of timelines and percentage of work completed. They don't take into consideration that these are not mutual linear events.

Have you ever heard of the 80/20 rule? Also known as the Pareto principle, it implies that roughly 80 percent of the effects of anything you might be doing come from 20 percent of the causes. In other words, for example, 80 percent of the work is likely generated by about 20 percent of the available workforce.

I'm not sure that this principal is true in today's business world. We expect a lot more from our teams and ourselves. If you aren't productive, you will probably be looking for a new job. I have an 80/20 rule of my own. 80%

of the work gets done in 20% of the time. Conversely, it takes 80% of the time to do the remaining 20% of the work. So if you are one week into a four week task and ask what percentage is complete and are told 50%, wouldn't you expect the remaining work to be completed in one more week? Is this the conclusion you could expect to take away from your status reports?

A better approach is to state a projects status based on work product completion. Is the task done? Yes or no. The task is binary; it either is or it is not, complete. Once a task is completed, you move to the next piece in the critical path gate. This allows you to point to where you are on the critical path and show what is the next effort along the way. Your gatekeepers should report to you on the worst/likely/best timeline for specific task. You should encourage them to resist the temptation to manage to the worst case. Focus on the most likely timeline and report based on achievement of required activities.

At this point you might be wondering what this has to do with stress. Remember, it's about time restraints. Time causes stress because people focus on the date and time something is done rather than the getting the thing done. When you remove the time constraint, surprisingly, things get done faster. You should ask your team leaders/gatekeepers to tell you when a task will be complete and hold them to it. They must inform you if they have a blocker that will effect the time they promised. Overall, the focus remains on getting the task completed.

Another area where stress comes into play is unreasonable expectations. People that don't understand the level of effort that is required to do a thing can often make assumptions of what can be achieved and when. You need to manage those expectations so that they are realistic and achievable within the constraints of time, resources and scope. By maintaining well-defined requirements along with a 3M process to validate those achievements, you can better control expectations.

CHAPTER 10

ARE WE THERE YET?

The few, the proud, the Marines. I have so many stories from my interactions with Marines, both from my time on active duty and in my post-military professional life. Most of these stories are too crude to be in a leadership book, but I needed to include at least one, because I think the lesson is a valuable one. Story time...

A group of young marines was sitting around a table in a bar in the port of Naples, Italy. It was about one in the morning and by this time everybody was getting trashed. There were some sailors and locals there as well, all of whom were likewise drinking heavily. As young marines often do, the boasting of their prowess was escalating as the night went on. One of the older marines started talking about being a badass. The discussion evolved into who was the biggest badass at the table. Then, as if an epiphany had occurred, one marine stands up and declares he has the way to decide who the biggest badass of all.

"Whoever can punch themselves in the face hardest, wins!"

They all agreed that this was a brilliant idea. None of them wanted to be seen as a wuss, so they all participated. Everyone in the bar was now quiet and started to gather around the five marines. They ordered a shot for each of them (Jägermeister, of course) to take after they had punched themselves in the face. And so it began. Each man trying to outdo the others. After the first round, they all decided they didn't have a clear winner. They ordered another shot and went in for round two. Then three and four.

On the fifth round, with the marines barely able to sit in their chairs, a Lance Corporal from Texas reached back and clocked himself. He hit himself so hard he was knocked out of his own chair. As he struggled to get up one of the other Marines noticed a tear rolling down his face and shouted, "Look- he's crying". It was at that point that they all agreed that the Lance Corporal won the competition, reasoning you had to be a serious badass to hit yourself so hard that you'd made yourself cry. Cheers went up, backs were slapped, and more drinks were ordered.

Standing next to me against the bar with the rest of the spectators was an older Marine. The Gunny Sargent looks at me and says, "What a wimp. Who cries when they hit themselves? Grow a pair."

Looking back on this story so many years after the fact has me thinking. If you hit yourself so hard that you cry, and enjoy it, does that make you a sadist or a masochist?

The lesson in this story is about the power of perception. Perception can trump reality.

A person's perception is their reality (true or not), unless you take action to rectify it. Here's how it works. There is science (or curse?) here. We're wired to identify and handle the complicated patterns of behaviors. It begins when these patterns are first created—from the very first appearance of the very first instance. In these moments, we quickly devise a hypothesis as to why the instance came to be, and how it fits into our world. Once this new perception is created, the brain starts looking for confirming data (conformational bias) that this is reality. In its search, the brain will accept all kinds of data as confirming data— regardless of whether it is, in fact, data based on reality.

So how can you get people to change their preconceived notions? Their perceptions are their realities, as are yours. The best method for rectifying this is by using a symbolic action. This is an activity or interaction taken that will demonstrate the values and priorities you want others to believe of you.

Here are some examples:
- Manage perception of how you value Time. How do you make time to demonstrate your highest priority? What meetings or events should do you attend? Are there opportunities to share messages or teach mini-lessons that would reinforce desired values? Are you present for both formal and informal gatherings? Think about how you will be perceived by these actions and decide what will promote the perceptions beneficial to you and your project.

- Manage perceptions on how you set Priorities. What is most important to the team? How can you align work, projects, and other initiatives to demonstrate what matters most? Are there previous priorities we can put aside in favor of higher value ones? Think about how you will be perceived by these actions and decide what will promote the perceptions beneficial to you and your project.

- Manage perceptions about your Ego: Are there times and/or places where I haven't walked the talk? Do I need to publicly acknowledge personal shortcomings? Have others coached me to become better? If so, how can I recognize their contributions? How can I demonstrate that even though I fall short, I keep on practicing to get better? Set the example and you will be managing the perception.

You also need to help others to learn how they are being

perceived and how to take steps to manage perceptions. A huge challenge with the nerds/geeks/deep thinker groups is they seldom see themselves as others do. It may be that they don't care- good for them- but in business, it might be required that they do. Managing how they are perceived will enable them to have less resistance toward achieving their objectives, and by extension, your goals.

In our vast toolbox of processes, methods and concepts that we use to un-f*ck the truly broken mess, perception management might well be the most valuable. It is a skill that needs to be practiced with mental intent. By that, I mean you need to *think* about what you want and then devise a plan of action and implement the plan. Don't just hope that your daily life sends the message that you want to be received. Act on it with intent and thoughtfulness. My dad once (or maybe a dozen times) told me, "Everything you say and everything you do has a direct reflection on you. It defines how people see you, defines who you are." Be sure that the image you project is the one that you want to be seen.

Speaking of our vast toolbox, let's think back on what we talked about. We've covered the importance of determining if a problem is real, how to define the problem, how to view probable causes and use a process of elimination to get to a most likely problem. We went through typical causes of programmatic and project-based management problems. We discussed the various and the diverse personnel challenges that you are likely to face and provided some tactics to get the results you're looking for.

Then we moved on to the most common root contributors to problems; Lack of proper communications, poor configuration and change management practices, and lack of basic project management skills. We talked about many issues that can cause challenges to projects success and went over some methods to overcome those challenges. Risk management, time management, the development of critical paths were all discussed.

In the end, we thought about our perceptions and how we are perceived by others and we examined some ways to manage the way we are viewed.

And so here we are, at the end.

As with all things, it's never over until the paperwork is done. We now find ourselves at Step 6. This step calls for documentation. The goal here is to develop lessons learned. It's supposed to be a retrospective on what went wrong, where the mistakes were made and what changes could be done in the future to ensure these issues don't happen on the next project.

The sad reality is that this step is often ignored. It means that you need to stand and be held accountable for actions that may have led to failure and discuss how to avoid the same mistakes in the future. Unfortunately, most people don't want to participate in these activities.

You still have a job to do, though. You need to make a report on your activities, discoveries, corrective actions and realized impacts. You will provide the empirical data you gathered and prove the changes created the desired outcomes. You will talk about the symptoms, problems, root causes and impacts. You will not mention names or positions; you're reporting on the activity you conducted as a Fixer, not placing blame. When you have completed the document, get your sponsor to sign off on it. You can make recommendations for project improvements at this time. Have I covered every situation that you might face? I'm sure I haven't, but the examples I have included are the ones I have most often faced and feel qualified to talk about. Is my way going to work for you? I hope so, but you will need to adapt solutions to your style and personality as well as the circumstances that you are dealing with. I've hit only lightly on some areas that need far more discussion than this book has room for. I highly recommend seeking out more books in areas that are new to you or you want to know more about.

There are two organizations that have a vast amount of information on many of these topics. The first is the Project Management Institute (pmi.org) and the other is the ITIL community (itlibrary.org).
I hope that you have enjoyed reading this book and found it entertaining and insightful. I had a great time writing it. I would greatly appreciate feedback and reviews.

ABOUT THE AUTHOR

Eric has been a project manager for over 30 years and brings his experience and humor to his writing. This is Eric's first book in what he hopes will be a popular series of leadership guides on fixing some of the most common business headaches. He lives with his wife, Tammy, dogs Molly & Max, and seriously crazy cat, Sybil in Woodbridge, Virginia. When he's not writing books, he loves travel, scuba diving and photography.

Coming Next:
The Help Desk Fixer
(preview begins on the following pages)

THE HELP DESK FIXER
A leadership Guide to creating an amazing IT support environment

Introduction

"I have a headache. I'm trying to run my business and every time I turn around I have to deal with employee complaints about their IT issues. I'm the CEO; I don't have time for this. Fix it NOW."

Sound familiar? I hear from CIO's all the time that more than all of the super technical challenges, it's their IT service/help desk issues that cause them the most stress. Let's face it. IT specialists like network and systems engineers, developers and database administrators are not known for their interactive skills in working with end users. To top it off, most end user issues are often viewed as petty irritations when compared to the technical challenges faced by these IT professionals. It's just not glamorous.

Rather than have these IT superstars working with end users, we create a help desk. A centralized IT service and support shop that's supposed to be a one-stop-shop for all your employee's IT service needs. But wait- there's more- Let's add in office moves, asset management, telecommunications needs, onboarding and off-boarding of employees, some facilities management stuff and maybe even conference room and Video Teleconferencing (VTC) services.

What happens in this environment is that the Help Desk becomes the producer of the image that is projected to the organization for the entire IT services department. What makes someone contact the help desk in the first place? Odds are the caller is frustrated, angry and stressed over an IT related issue. It can be something small or complex. It doesn't matter, because to the end user, at that moment, it's the most important thing in their life. How the help desk person answers the phone and treats that end user will be the direct reflection on the professionalism, capabilities and quality of your entire IT organization. A positive experience can lend to enduring high respect and appreciation developed over time. A negative experience can ruin everything you've done in an instance.

If all of this is true, then why are help desk services one of the lowest compensated categories in the IT services industry? If so much rides on the quality of a service desk staff, why then, do we value them so lowly? When a help desk is underperforming, the impact is wide spread. It creates a lack of trust in the organization. It spawns an environment of employee complaining. It creates a convenient excuse for anything that doesn't get done. It contributes to low employee morale and high attrition.

When an IT help desk (or service desk) is staffed with well-trained customer support specialists, using processes, workflows and escalations that result in rapid resolutions of user complaints, the view is completely different. Having a cheerful, helpful person answer the phone when you are at your wits end can defuse frustration and anger with IT services and create a positive result. When employees are happy with their IT services, they feel empowered to focus on their work. Employees are generally happier with everything when their IT services are excellent. Attrition is reduced and employee referrals go up.

So, why is it that so many CIO's are faced with the problem of underperforming help desk services? The answer is complex. The solution might just be you, the Help Desk Fixer.

CHAPTER 1:
CUSTOMER SATISFACTION TRUTH

For many years, the end-user survey was the measurement tool to gauge the quality of IT services in an organization. In many cases it still is. Early in my career, I made an interesting discovery. I was reviewing a stack of survey results and noticed a trend. One of my deskside support people was getting great survey results while some others, well, not so much. As I dug deeper into the survey questions and answers, I noticed something really confusing.

Survey responses were on a 1 to 5 scale where 1 was poor and 5 was excellent. Questions were about the specific and general experience the end user had in their engagement with the technician. One of the ratings was Overall Satisfaction. This was, to me, the most important rating of all. But there was another really important question: Did the technician resolve the problem? This was a simple yes or no question. So why was one technician receiving almost all "5" ratings for overall satisfaction when they had a less than 25% "yes" responses in the question of if the problem was resolved? Even more confusing was that the four other techs were receiving an average of 3.2 overall satisfaction ratings with over 90% "yes" on problem resolution. If they were solving more problems, how on earth were the customers giving them *lower* satisfaction ratings? I decided to investigate further.

I picked up the surveys and went in search of the end users that filled them out. I told them that I appreciated the time that they took to complete the surveys and asked if they would be willing to answer some follow up questions. My most important question was "why did you select the overall satisfaction rating that you gave?" For the four technicians that had a 3.2 average, the responses were varied but similar. The feeling was that although they fixed the issue in a timely manner, they acted like it was a stupid problem. They gave the end user (aka customer) the impression that they had much better things to do than help them and made them feel almost ashamed for asking for help in the first place.

When I spoke with the very satisfied customers and asked why they gave such a high rating if their problem wasn't resolved, they responded in an entirely different way. "Bob (we'll call him that) was wonderful. He was cheerful. We chatted for a bit as he asked me about the issue. He showed genuine concern that my issue was important to him. He told me about others who had the same problem and how frustrated they were. Even though he didn't have a resolution, he told me he was getting someone who could fix the issue and was putting it at the top of his priorities list."

Wow. It seems that if you're a good technician and fix a lot of problems, you're not going to get high satisfaction ratings if you're not a nice person. If you're an average, or even less than average, troubleshooter, but you're a really nice person, you can get really great customer satisfaction ratings. Go figure.

It turns out satisfaction ratings had little to do with whether a problem was fixed or not. But wasn't it important to fix the problem? Wasn't the ability to restore the working capabilities of the IT service the primary goal? Isn't that the JOB of the IT services professional? Of course it is. But the point is this: You can be a great technical engineer and stink as a customer support specialist. You can be a great customer support specialist and stink as a technician. It is a rare gift to have both qualities in the same person. They are out there, but not in enough quantities to go around.

Maybe you are a fortunate Help Desk Manager and have found a few of these super-amazing customer service oriented skilled technicians. Be happy, but don't think it will last very long. People with these skills tend to move on to more technical challenges pretty quickly. Frankly, we, as leaders, should encourage them to do so. Not to mentor and support their efforts to advance their IT career would be a disservice and reflect poorly on your leadership skills.

It is for this reason that you have two things you must

focus on quickly. Teach customer service skills to your good technicians, and mentor the technical skills of your good customer service staff. As "The Help Desk Fixer", the very first thing you need to do is gauge the level of satisfaction of the general user population. You might be thinking that surveys are a great tool for that, and the certainly have their place. But we already assume that there is a problem here. That's why the helped desk needs to be "fixed".

To really understand the issues with a dissatisfied user base, you must listen to the end users. You need to become the person that everyone will view a caring leader, focused on identify problems and producing resolutions. Someone fixated on improving the over IT experience for the entire organization. Someone who delivers results, not just words. You need to take charge of customer's perceptions, and drive it to the vision that the C-level leadership is expecting.

If you have been brought in to be a fixer, you are more than just a manager of staff. You have been hired for skills beyond signing timesheets and doing performance evaluations. You will be expected to hire and fire, promote and mentor. But most of all, you are expected to identify the problems that are behind the symptoms that appear as dissatisfaction. You cannot sit in an office behind a desk all day. You have to be visible, dynamic and available.

You need to get up off of your backside and go meet people. Were co-located, walk around to the different business groups. Make sure you take a note pad or tablet. Introduce yourself. Talk to a few people in each area. Ask them a few questions about their ideas on IT services. Write down their names and their comments. Ask leading questions, like "what do you think about... or how do you feel about..." that require more than a yes or no response. Let them know that you are here because your sponsor (CIO, CEO, whoever it is) has a sincere interest in improving the overall IT services and support. Ask if they have any current issues that the Help Desk could support them with. If they do, help them open a support ticket right then and there. Note the ticket and follow up personally. You are creating an image, a perception of who you are.

It's important at this point to focus on the typical staff members. The folks in leadership roles are important too, but when you talk to them you want to be able to report your experiences with their staff. Let them know you have started the process to improve services. You want to let them know that you are the "single throat to choke" in the event that they are dissatisfied with IT support services. You are the escalation point and you will resolve any issues.

In situations where you are not co-located, it is best if you can travel to and visit staff members in person. If that's not possible, phone calls must suffice. In the beginning few weeks, visiting users must be a daily activity for you. How many users that are supported will determine how many you should talk with daily. In a work week, you must ensure that you have spoken with people in every department within the organization supported by your help desk. In weeks two and three, you need to be speaking to leaders; branch chiefs, division heads and department level executives. Respect their time, but introduce yourself to everyone with the same message. You are committed to IT service improvement and things are going to get better.

You might feel like you're setting yourself up as a knight in shining armor, here to save the day. That is true, to some extent, but must be an unspoken innuendo. Let people draw their own conclusions, because you will begin shifting the focus of attention away from yourself soon. What you are trying to establish here is that you are a mature tested professional. You are responsible and you take action. You are a new person that is going to listen, care and be responsive to the concerns of the end users. You are creating the first pieces of a new customer service attitude that is focused by the entire IT support staff. You are going to improve overall customer satisfaction.

"The Help Desk Fixer" is coming in spring of 2020 and will be available at Amazon. Watch for it!

Printed in Great Britain
by Amazon